Leadership
on **Purpose**

To my daughters Jessica, Giselle, Sophia, and especially
my husband Ric, with love.

To Margaret S. Fortune, my wife. To Margaret G. Fortune,
my daughter. To Rex Fortune, III, my son. To Gwen Fortune-Blakely,
my "first born." And to Lenora Simone Blakely, my first grandchild.

Leadership

Promising Practices for African American and Hispanic Students

on Purpose

Rosemary Papalewis 🖋 Rex Fortune

CORWIN PRESS, INC.
A Sage Publications Company
Thousand Oaks, California

For information:

Corwin Press, Inc.
A Sage Publications Company
2455 Teller Road
Thousand Oaks, California 91320
www.corwinpress.com

Sage Publications Ltd.
6 Bonhill Street
London EC2A 4PU
United Kingdom

Sage Publications India Pvt. Ltd.
M-32 Market
Greater Kailash I
New Delhi 110 048 India

Printed in the United States of America

Library of Congress Cataloging-in-Publication Data

Papalewis, Rosemary.
  Leadership on purpose: Promising practices for African American and Hispanic students / Rosemary Papalewis, Rex Fortune.
    p. cm.
Includes bibliographical references and index.
  ISBN 0-7619-4547-4
  ISBN 0-7619-4548-2 (pbk.)
  1. African Americans—Education. 2. Hispanic Americans—Education. 3. Education, Urban—United States. 4. Educational leadership—United States. I. Fortune, Rex. II. Title.
  LC2717 .P36 2002
  371.829'96073—dc21

                        2002006453

This book is printed on acid-free paper.

    03 04 05 10 9 8 7 6 5 4 3 2

Acquisitions Editor:	Robb Clouse
Editorial Assistant:	Erin Clow
Copy Editor:	Annette Pagliaro
Production Editor:	Denise Santoyo
Typesetter:	Siva Math Setters, Chennai, India
Indexer:	Kathy Paparchontis
Cover Designer:	Tracy E. Miller
Production Artist:	Sandra Ng

Contents

Acknowledgments   ix

About the Authors   xi

1. Promising Practices   1

2. Principal Strategies   11
   Clarity of Mission   12
      PP: Posting of School Mission   12
      PP: Bulletin Boards Are Tied to
         the Standards   13
      PP: Principal Spends First Few Weeks of
         School in Classrooms Daily   14
   Schoolwide Scheduling of Activities   14
      PP: Lunch Period Is 45 Minutes Long
         With Only One 20-Minute Recess to
         Optimize Teacher Sharing   15
      PP: No interruptions Before 10:30 A.M.
         to Allow a Reading Block   15
      PP: Pacing Schedules Are Done Schoolwide
         and Are Reviewed by the Principal Weekly   15
      PP: Class Size Reduction Through 4th Grade   16
   Other Scheduling and Curricula Priorities   17
   Summary   18

3. School Curriculum and Classroom Instruction   19
   Assessment   20
      PP: Principal Tests New Students   21
      PP: Student Portfolios as Continuous
         Assessment   22
   Staff Development   23

PP: Teachers Are Trained in English
    Language Development (ELD)   25
Teacher Collaboration   27
    PP: Teachers Hold Regular Team Meetings   28
Instruction   29
    PP: Direct-Instruction Approach Is Used   30
    PP: English Language Development (ELD)
    Is Taught Schoolwide   31
    PP: A Pre-K Program Is Organized   32
    PP: Daily Lessons Are Posted in
    the Classroom   33
Summary   34

4. Family and Community Connections   35
School–Home Communication   36
    PP: Students Wear Uniforms   37
    PP: Correspondence to Parents Is Sent in
    More Than One Language   38
    PP: Schools Provide Free Breakfast   39
School Activities in the Home   40
    PP: Homework Is Assigned   40
    PP: Schools Provide Assistance for Parents   41
    PP: Students Are Assigned Work
    During Intersession   43
Parents in Schools   43
    PP: Parents Are Involved in Schools   44
    PP: Parents Are Trained to Assist in
    the Classroom   45
    PP: School Curriculum Includes Parents   46
Summary   47

5. From Promising Practices to Action   49
What We Need to Ask Ourselves   50
    Questions for School-Site Leaders   50
    About School Leadership   50
    About the School Curriculum   51
    About the Classroom   51
    About the Community   52
    Questions for Teachers   53
    About School Leadership   53
    About the School Curriculum   54

About the Classroom   54
About the Community   55
Questions for District Administrators   55
About District Leadership   55
About School Leadership   56
About the Curriculum and Classrooms   56
About the Community   57
Questions for School Board Members   57
About School Leadership   58
About the School Curriculum   58
About the Classroom   58
About the Community   59
Questions for Parents   59
About School Leadership   59
About the School Curriculum   60
About the Classroom   60
About the Community   60
Summary   61

Resource A: School-Site Information   63

Resource B: Brief Overview of Bibliography   65

Resource C: Research Methodology   69

Resource D: A Case for District Leadership   77

References   83

Suggested Readings   87

Index   89

Acknowledgments

The authors express appreciation to Project Pipeline for its support for the field study, which was the basis for this publication. The Executive Director, Mrs. Margaret Fortune, provided the resources to support this study. She also provided clerical assistance associated with the logistics of moving the visiting team around the state to conduct the study.

Appreciation is extended to those who visited schools, wrote reports, and served as a focus group to analyze our findings at the conclusion of each day of work. These included Dr. Lois Ortmann, Ms. Audrey Lytle, Mr. Tom Wright, Mrs. Lois Ford, Ms. Luella Harris, Ms. Stephanie Smith, Ms. Addie Ellis, Mr. Al Ramey, and the authors.

Special appreciation goes to two veteran principals, who had retired shortly before our study began. Both Mrs. Nancy Ichinaga and Mrs. Marge Thompson were principals for 26 years at the Bennett-Kew Elementary and Kelso Elementary Schools, respectively. Both of these Inglewood Unified School District principals provided an in-depth interview with the authors and suggested others in the district that we contacted for visitations or interviews.

We are most appreciative of the time and hospitality provided by principals, teachers, and staff members at the schools visited. These included: Mrs. Lorraine Fong, Principal of the Bennett-Kew Elementary School; Mrs. Jacqueline Moore, Principal of the Kelso Elementary School; Mrs. Betty Jo Steward, Principal of the Highland Elementary School; Mrs. Debbie Tate, Principal of the Payne Elementary School; Mrs. Marie Stricklin, Principal of the Parent Elementary

School; Dr. Norma Baker, Principal of the Hudnall Elementary School; Mr. Michael Edelman, former Principal of the Hudnall Elementary School; and all of the Inglewood Unified School District. We thank Mrs. Cathleen McLane, Principal of the Kaiser Elementary School; Ms. Donna Wilson, Principal of the Grass Valley Elementary School; and Mr. Ron Lay, Principal of the Howard Elementary School; and all of the Oakland Unified School District. We also thank Dr. Ernie Roy, Principal of King-Drew Medical Magnet High School; Ms. Sue Wong, Principal of Lane Elementary School; and Ms. Joyce Dixon; Principal of Cowan Elementary School in the Los Angles Unified School District. Finally, we thank Mrs. Carolyn Horsley, Principal of Imperial Elementary School in the Downey Unified School District.

The authors would not have been able to execute the myriad tasks associated with conducting a statewide field study involving participants from various locations without the administrative assistance of Lynette Roby, Project PIPELINE, Gloria Kluge from Center Unified School District, and Kim Shaw and Tim Cochrane, from the Center for Teaching and Learning, California State University, Sacramento. Reading and proofing the document were supported by Mr. Steven O'Donnell and Ms. Melva Arditti. Of special note is the time and attention given to our writing efforts by author Dr. Concha Delgado-Gaitan, who supported us in our efforts to turn our research into a book.

About
the Authors

 **Rosemary Papalewis** is Professor of Educational Leadership and Policy Studies at California State University, Sacramento (CSUS), and serves as the Director of the University's Center for Teaching and Learning, working with faculty across all disciplines and colleges. Prior to coming to CSUS, she held positions as the Western Region Vice President for Sylvan Learning Systems, the Assistant Vice Chancellor for InterInstitutional Relations for the California State University System, and Professor and Co-Founding Director for the Joint Doctoral Program in Educational Leadership of California State University, Fresno, and the University of California. She has also served as a teacher at the K–12 level (California), and as Principal and Chief Administrator (private schools in Nebraska).

Papalewis is a Past President of both the National Association of Professors of Educational Administration and the California Association of Professors of Educational Administration (two terms). She recently ended her term representing the California State University as Vice-Chair and Commissioner on the California Student Aid Commission and Board Chair of the Commission's auxiliary, EdFund, a $2.2 billion student-lending service. Papalewis actively serves as a consultant to school districts, California National Guard youth programs, and corporate (both for-profit and nonprofit) educational companies. She is an active researcher, having published and presented in the areas of K–12 and higher education leadership, joint doctoral programs, teacher training, mentoring, women in administration, and, most recently, technology in university teaching.

Rex Fortune is District Superintendent in the Center Unified School District in Sacramento County. He has served as a Public School District Superintendent in California for the past 18 years, including in the Inglewood Unified School District, an urban district in Los Angeles County with over 20,000 pupils, preschool through adult education. His current district has doubled in size since Fortune first arrived more than a dozen years ago, transforming from a rural district to a suburban district with 5,500 pupils preschool through high school. Formerly, Fortune was Associate Superintendent in the California State Department of Education for more than a decade, where his program responsibilities ranged from State Director of Compensatory Education to manager for Gifted and Talented Education. Fortune served as the State Superintendent's representative to State Board Committees responsible for Vocational Education and Equal Educational Opportunities. He was also the state's representative to a number of statewide professional organizations.

Among his proudest accomplishments is the passage of a local general obligation bond for the Center District for $59 million for the construction of new facilities, where teachers and students use state-of-the-art technology. He was also instrumental in the creation and use of the district's strategic plan to guide instructional improvement, especially reading instruction at elementary and secondary schools. Fortune also helped create Project PIPELINE, a nonprofit educational services organization directed by Margaret Fortune that has recruited, trained, and credentialed more than 200 teachers for 14 school districts in Alameda and Sacramento Counties over the past 7 years.

1

Promising Practices

D o principals and teachers intend for all students to learn? Of course. Can we demonstrate that all students successfully learn? Maybe. An elementary school principal described successful practices as, "I wrote the schoolwide objectives. Tied them to the reading/language arts and mathematics textbook objectives . . . and state standards . . . and tied the teacher-evaluation process to the schoolwide objectives. Helping students to achieve, and holding teachers responsible for doing so, is very purposeful."

This principal identified a practice he uses and believes is responsible for his high student achievement. This practice is called "purposeful and intended leadership." Who, how, and why we ask (site leaders, teachers, parents, district administrators, and school board members) become critical to the choices we make, what we accept, and the ways we begin to change teacher and principal practices.

The "purposeful leader" described in this book comes from schools of high poverty and high achievement with students of color. These successful principals portray their schools as challenging.

"[I] deal with the reality of strong unions, urban city bureaucracy."

"My community is gang-infested with frequent shootings occurring all around the school."

"Many of my parents are foster parents caring for drug babies."

This book "purposely intends" to close the gap between students who learn and those who do not, and provide helpful strategies for educators to reflect on practices that support high student achievement for students of color.

Our research identified 13 schools, listed in Resource A, that exhibited high achievement for two populations that traditionally do not perform well on standardized tests. These 13 schools displayed strong administrative leadership *that was tied* to a high degree of attention to instructional practices. Teachers and administrators fostered high expectations, such as one principal who stated, "Leave no student behind."

The schools were safe and orderly (even in the most extreme urban settings) and *were especially* not rigid. Pupil progress was frequently monitored and focused on curriculum standards tied to statewide assessments. "I accept no excuses," said one principal. Pupil acquisition of basic school skills such as reading, writing, and mathematics (elementary) took precedence over all other school activities. Another principal said, "I was reprimanded for not having my students participate in a local community writing contest. There is too much fluff that we are asked to do." These practices, although not all new, were done with a consistency of purpose—to promote higher student achievement, especially with African American and Hispanic students.

Harsh statements about the viability of public education abound. It is an increasingly common complaint that schools do not prepare their students for the rigors of the workplace. Many hard-working educators have attempted to implement well-intended policies to ameliorate the devastating educational conditions in all schools—suburban, rural, and urban—with only minimal results. Dismal results on educational achievement tests, especially for African American and Hispanic students, continue to frustrate public school educators.

Today's educational system doesn't need more reforms imposed on top of the existing top-down bureaucratic policies that straightjackets schools, leaders, teachers, and students. What it does require is dynamic, organic change inside out and bottom up, where local schools and communities are involved in shaping their own goals and outcomes.

This book recognizes the imperative of critical "purpose-intended" leadership, which takes into account the school principal's leadership responsibilities, his or her ability to vigorously assess the social and cultural environment, and then collaboratively devise practices that engage teachers, students and parents to achieve high-expectation standards for all students. "Good principals know how to be leaders to [their] teachers; how to be analytical with student data," a teacher said.

The outcomes noted as Promising Practices (PP) in this book refer to high performance on the part of all students on standardized exams. A brief literature review and bibliography on effective school practices and principals as instructional leaders can be found in Resource B.

Today we all wrestle with determining an acceptable number of students in a particular school or district who can be allowed to fail (not all students try equally), and acknowledging the role of poverty and color in this mind-set. Because families do not predetermine which child will be allowed to fail, why then are schools apparently willing to act as if some failure is acceptable, and, worse, expected (such as those in the lowest quartile on statewide testing)? "We have neither extra money nor business partnerships. . . . We do have high teacher turnover and high numbers of emergency permit teachers. . . . All of these could be called excuses. . . . We succeed because we don't accept such excuses," said a principal.

The Promising Practices identified in this book are strategies that principals and teachers used with all students. These have been identified as "intended" practices that have led to their success with students. "We see a need [and ask] how are we going to address this need," said a teacher. These observed practices with Hispanic and African American students represent strategies that we consider replicable. They made a defining difference for the 13 high-performing and high-minority (African American and Hispanic) schools we studied. A detailed methodology section for the research can be found in Resource C.

Originally, five schools were visited. These schools were chosen based on a statewide ranking used in California, called the Academic Performance Index (API). Baseline data were established in 1999 using the API, establishing a statewide ranking of every public school based on the SAT-9 tests administered in grades two through eleven. The highest number rank of ten to the lowest number rank of one identified 50% of the schools in California as failing.

Among these failing schools are an inordinately large proportion serving students of color. The number of schools that were 51% or more African American or Hispanic ranking ten, nine, or eight were relatively few at all levels—elementary, junior, and senior high. The first five schools visited were schools that were high minority and ranked eight, nine, or ten (California Department of Education, 2001).

Failing schools have long been associated with character-istics explaining their failure (high poverty, high minority, poorly trained teachers, high staff turnover, etc.). These five urban and suburban schools with a majority of students of color displayed an unusual commonality of practices.

Two major themes emerged: structured, high-expectation practices and manipulation of the length of day and school year to maximize study time for students who need it.

Eight additional schools were visited that matched the original criteria of the first five schools (API ranking was dropped to above the median of six so that additional schools of color could be found at the junior and senior high levels). The purpose was to identify the common practices of principals, teachers, and parents to achieve high success with Hispanic and African American students. Under the two major themes previously mentioned, we identified additional Promising Practices for schools to consider using with these two specific and distinct populations:

- Direct instruction methods utilized
- Frequent and multiple levels of assessment practices by teachers and principals
- Test-taking strategies taught and practiced throughout the year
- Solid teacher-to-teacher communication across grade levels and departments
- Teachers know the expected state standards and tie them to lesson plans
- Students are expected to respect teachers

All the Promising Practices identified as successful strategies by those we interviewed in these 13 high-performing schools with 51% or more African American and/or Hispanic students were then applied to the elementary level. The *structured, high-expectation* theme practices for elementary schools were:

- Students in elementary grades are tested immediately in reading and math by the principal, with parents present for possible reclassification when they first enroll in school.
- Reading/language arts time is protected, uninterrupted instructional time. Mornings are structured to optimize language arts and math study.
- Pacing schedules are done schoolwide and are reviewed by the principal weekly.
- A "Junior" first grade is created for kindergarten students not ready for first grade. It is a full day (counted for ADA) with a possible double promotion in 5th grade.
- Teachers and coaches collaborate weekly to ensure all tests and homework are the same by grade level and to share best practices. This leadership team collects and reviews all student assessment data.
- Teacher lesson plans are tied to their evaluation, which is tied to their teaching the SAT-9 objectives and standards. All coaches and teachers turn in lesson plans weekly to the principal.

- Teachers, by grade level, disaggregate student data by subgroup populations.
- Portfolio assessments are passed on year to year with examples of beginning skill and expert skill demonstrated.
- Uniforms are required or expected—as a high expectation for student behavior. (All schools visited have strong faculty unions.)
- All teachers are trained and practice ELD (English Language Development) strategies. Pullouts are limited to only the afternoon or individual reading portion of Open Court.
- PEP (Proficiency in English Practice) used for African American students to speak Standard English—daily drills, and monthly assemblies.
- Mission of the school is posted in classrooms and the office.
- Objectives are posted on whiteboards/chart paper for daily lessons.
- Bulletin boards are tied to the standards.
- Saxon math and Open Court used for direct-instruction approach. Waterford software program used in kindergarten and 1st grade for remediation and parent education. Scholastic READ 180 used in 4th to 8th grades for remediation.
- Principals and vice principals do recess duty for teachers, where union agreement has been reached.
- Principal is fully trained in the reading/language and math programs used.
- Assessment is a continuous disaggregating of data on multiple levels, as is use of portfolios.
- Free breakfast during testing weeks of SAT-9.
- Parents are given assistance on how to check homework and help their child to do the homework. Grade-level meetings are held for parents. Parents have copies of the standards.
- Parent programs include helping students succeed, hands-on curriculum training taught by classroom

teacher, and training in test-taking strategies for their children—training includes expectation that parents will be able to help in classrooms. And, of course, all notes home are done in multiple languages.

A second major theme, *manipulate the length of day and school year to maximize time for students who need it,* was identified with the following practices for elementary schools:

- Kindergarten is extended by 45 minutes to one hour for lower-achieving students by the classroom teacher.
- Assess pre-K children in May and give them a readiness-for-school packet to work on in the summer.
- Alternately, have a pre-K program twice a week for a year before kindergarten.
- Before SAT-9 testing, entire school is on an extended schedule for one to two months (adds 45 minutes to each day).
- Extended day for 5th graders, all year, four days a week (K–5 school).
- Class size reduction through 4th grade.
- Schoolwide homework five nights including uniform reading lessons.
- Intersession is not considered a vacation. Students come to school for 2½ hours for tutoring—four times/week, taught by instructional aides. The classes are ability grouped. Or homework packets are sent home and are checked upon returning from intersession. Teachers create the intersession packets tied to SAT-9 objectives and the standards.
- New students are enrolled in intersession to admit in the next track for a jump start on their studies.
- Lunch period is 45 minutes long with only one 20-minute recess to optimize teacher sharing (union districts).
- Mornings are all reading and language arts tied to social studies and science.
- Early dismissal one day a week (25 minutes) for team meetings.

- Grade-level teachers plan together (homework and benchmarks) in times during the school day provided and agreed to by the administration and unions.

Only three schools, two K–8 and one senior high school (magnet), with 51% or more African American and/or Hispanic students, were visited. Practices teachers and administrators identified were:

- Uniforms are required.
- Principal is especially visible.
- Parents are involved in SAT preparation.
- Teachers/principal/parents trained with students by Kaplan for SAT prep. These preparation strategies are woven into daily lesson plans throughout the curriculum.
- Daily uninterrupted and sustained reading for 15 minutes.
- Content standards posted in each classroom.
- Portfolios are kept for all students.
- Counselor on site, who also works on community services.
- Suggestion box for students. Principal responds to each suggestion, every 2 weeks, and publishes the entire list.
- Scheduling fits needs of courses, students, and teachers for maximum flexibility.
- No early release for juniors and seniors.
- Full-time technologist to service computers.
- Classrooms, library, and hallways have abundant displays celebrating diversity by subject area.

From this total list, we chose 24 practices found in most of the schools to expand on in further detail. These are arranged into three broad categories: principal strategies, school curriculum and classroom instruction, and family and community connections. Chapter 2 details seven leadership practices for principals; Chapter 3 details eight curriculum and classroom instruction practices; Chapter 4 focuses on nine family and community connections; and Chapter 5 moves from the Promising Practices to other issues that require exploration.

All the practices observed were, of course, not found at all the schools. We have listed all of them in the hopes that some will matter more to you than others. However, it is important to note that participants at the 13 schools all wanted to emphasize that it was in the *totality* of parent, teacher, and principal practices that led to their achievements. (Note: A decision was made not to use any of the specific names of the principals, teachers, parents, or staff interviewed. Only where public data are explained is the information explicit.)

Somewhat surprising to us was that only a few of the practices are specific to Hispanic or African American children. We did not find a lot of culturally specific instructional materials or activities. To paraphrase most of the 13 principals, "Don't think Hispanic, African American, and so on. Think children." Another said, "[There is] no real evidence of 'people of color' stuff. All kids can learn." And another said, "Knowledge is power . . . [All students] can [learn] because they think they can."

These principals and teachers believed that, as one stated, "Sharing and caring is how we (student, teacher, principal) feel about our school." Because they were high-minority schools, when we asked what specific curriculum programs they used, we were told, "Use an integrated curriculum. Research knowledge about how children learn." Another principal said, "We rearranged our sequence of math classes based on our experience and recommendations from Jaime Escalante. [A movie, *Stand and Deliver,* was made about this former mathematics teacher from LAUSD.] It made more sense for the students."

Hispanic and African American culture was readily identified through bulletin boards and hallways vividly displaying faces of color. In the upper grades and high school, discipline-specific posters of color were very apparent. A male African American high school principal said, "My magnet school attracts more girls. I am constantly in classrooms . . . because they [boys] need positive male role models." A Hispanic principal said, "Failure is not an option, especially for my kids. I accept no excuses." Principals try to hire teachers of color, though many of these schools are staffed with high numbers of Emergency Permit teachers.

We hope this book serves as a lightning rod for planning and implementing winning directions for students of color. We look to our school leadership to access, define, and create Promising Practices by which students can flourish to their potential.

Often it is said it's not the schools' problem that kids can't learn. Fault is blamed on the loss of the family nucleus, the fact that schools have students for little more than five learning hours a day, the overexposure to violence through television, and so on.

However, some of these schools housed 800 to 900 students. They were asphalt, high-fenced, no-grass school sites situated on less than two acres of land, and directly in the flight pattern of Los Angeles International Airport, where planes land incessantly during the daytime hours. These schools had no open walkways bordering the streets and community housing due to gangs, drugs, and violence in the neighborhood. Our arrival at one school was timed to have armed guards in the parking lot to safely escort us into the school because rival gangs (Bloods and Crips) border the school street corners.

How we purposefully arrange curriculum and motivate teachers focused on student achievement requires school leaders to question all their schooling practices. Today, most states tie curriculum standards to assessment tests to ensure that educators must disaggregate data in ways not previously done in our schools. Effective school leaders need to be risk takers. We have focused on Promising Practices that have proven to be effective in the schools we observed. It is important to note that testing itself may have inherent flaws tied to standards that are not supported by current textbooks or specific teaching practices. Albeit, we have combined Promising Practices with the commitment of these schools to be organized for the purpose of everyone learning *and to demonstrate this intention.* As a consequence, these schools have yielded high results through test scores. We quickly realized that this point was perhaps the strongest case that could be made in support of public education and in proposing a direction that works.

2

Principal Strategies

School leadership has historic authority dating back to Horace Mann and his idea of school-site governance. The school leader of today knows that accountability for every child is more critical than ever. For over 40 years now, researchers have found high-achieving classrooms, schools, and, more recently, districts where poor and minority students have been effectively taught to read and compute as evidenced by their scores on various tests.

The decision to lead can be made on many different levels. But one thing is certain: Leadership comes with responsibilities and accountabilities. To bring about change, leaders within schools need to quantify effective ideas or strategies that increase people's abilities to think freshly about the situations they find themselves in and to help implement informed policies and practices based on student learning. When you decide to become a leader, you think and act differently. Principal responsibilities that make a difference in changing schools need to be documented as the 21st century begins and the fate of public education looms in almost daily news headlines.

In this study, we found that principals had specific practices that they consciously instituted for the purpose of enforcing a strong presence in the school. As was stated earlier, these practices, although not all new, were done with a consistency of purpose—to promote higher student achievement by removing the variables to enable students and teachers to do their best. The Promising Practices that were evident at most of the schools include the following: Principals post the school mission all around the school; tie bulletin boards to the standards; spend the first few weeks in classrooms daily; provide a 45-minute lunch period with only one 20-minute recess to optimize teacher sharing; insist on class size reduction through 4th grade; and principals and/or vice-principals do recess and lunch duty for/with teachers.

For example, one elementary school principal not only believed that change was possible but that it was also a collective effort. She told her staff, "If I'm going to change the educational setting, then I have to accomplish it with every one of you. Your total power and effectiveness are part of my own feelings." This school was ranked a "9" and was the only African American majority school that ranked that high in the state on the baseline API score. There were no majority African American schools ranked a "10" on the baseline API scores in 1999.

Another example was an African American high school principal of a Los Angeles magnet school who expressed leadership as, "We must share the same vision as the staff."

CLARITY OF MISSION

Above all, leadership and stewardship in a school mandate the development of a clear mission. This does not mean that only the principal is aware of the mission statement. It means that as a school leader, the principal must involve everyone in the school in recognizing, enforcing, and implementing the mission statement. The statement must become a daily concrete objective.

PP: Posting of School Mission

The principals in the schools we studied made the mission "Learning for All" more than a lofty statement that gets bound up and sits on the bookshelf in the front office. As one elementary school principal stated, "We have goals [tied to the mission] posted in each classroom. Daily goals are posted. Goal setting is spoken about a lot to staff, students, and parents." This strong proclamation does not mean that all children can learn at the same rate on the same day in the same way. To make this mission statement a working blueprint, the principals at the schools we studied ensure that everyone knows what the schools stand for and what their directions are. Management alone will not ensure success of the mission. Everyone needs to share in understanding, believing, and being reminded of it daily if they are to participate in accomplishing it. Together they share the responsibility for the educational plan.

Principals with a strong commitment to their school's mission ensure that everyone identified with the school is aware of and fully committed to the school's direction.

PP: Bulletin Boards Are Tied to the Standards

Performance and learning standards are goals everyone in the school needs to be continually reminded of if they are to be held accountable for meeting them. In and out of the classroom, teachers, students, and parents stay informed through the literature and notices that are posted on the bulletin boards in classrooms and school corridors. Visual displays reflecting the curriculum being taught reinforce both teaching and learning for everyone in the classroom (especially when tied to the lessons of that particular week, not just for seasons or holidays). Having both a daily and weekly outline helps students focus on what the teacher is translating from state standards. The bulletin board is one modality that all the schools we visited utilized to the advantage of student learning. Principals set high expectations that were linked to optimizing the use of bulletin boards.

Standards need to be ample, yet specific enough to be meaningful and attainable. Of course, it makes matters worse when educators demand that all students at a given grade level must be able to perform a certain task. This guarantees that some students will be branded as failures because they do not learn at the same pace as their peers. Bulletin boards we observed were clearly tied to the curriculum, linking several subjects through words, pictures, and activities. These bulletin boards were an outcome strategy used to focus on the curriculum. As one elementary school principal explained, "Teachers' evaluation objectives are tied to goals for meeting standards . . . bulletin boards included."

PP: Principal Spends First Few Weeks of School in Classrooms Daily

An elementary school principal says, "What keeps me out of the classroom is all the special education [meetings]. I'm always at an IEP (Individual Educational Plan) meeting." Apart from that, like other principals, she is found observing teachers and students in their classroom.

Principals agree, "You need to be in the classroom to see what's going on—give feedback." The one thing that makes observing classrooms more difficult is that many principals do not have a vice principal. When teachers and students are accustomed to seeing the principal frequently in their classroom, they feel supported, and communication between them extends beyond the discipline level. Another elementary school principal visits each classroom two to three times a week, covers classes if no substitute is available, and provides feedback to the teacher. This principal does three observations per teacher each year.

SCHOOLWIDE SCHEDULING OF ACTIVITIES

Nowhere is the industrial model of schooling more obvious than in the schools' use of time. Under the industrial model, the time is fixed so that production is optimized. Rigid schedules are fixed from the district office. The length of the school year, school day, even class periods are set by law, with every student getting exactly the same amount of time. Through innovations such as quality flexible time arrangements, learning becomes the end. Scheduling is no longer an end in itself. Specific Promising Practices in the elementary schools we studied supplied teachers and students with more quality time together. A K–8 elementary school principal stated, "Whenever I'm free, I'm in a class. My people [administrators] do that too."

PP: Lunch Period Is 45 Minutes Long With Only One 20-Minute Recess to Optimize Teacher Sharing

As a way of breaking out of the straightjacket, principals in the schools we studied stretched the instructional time by minimizing interruptions in instruction. Continuity of instruction is prioritized over the traditional structure of a 10-minute recess twice a day. Teachers appreciated not having to disengage from their lessons. In the elementary schools (K–8) we visited, the administration and teachers have arranged their instructional time to promote uninterrupted class time.

PP: No Interruptions Before 10:30 A.M. to Allow a Reading Block

Learning in school is a function of time. Traditionally, most schools are organized in a way that pays more respect to seat time than to how students learn. Therefore, schools have had to reorganize their time to create meaningful blocks of "learning time."

In all of the elementary schools we visited, the principals held to the rule that no one will interrupt the classroom during the reading period—no bells, no intercom announcements, no one dropping off a lunch. A principal stated, "[I] protect instructional time as sacred."

PP: Pacing Schedules Are Done Schoolwide and Are Reviewed by the Principal Weekly

Principals with control of their schoolwide activities are not only at the pulse of all the school events but also are able to schedule their presence in key activities. A key activity is the evaluation of teachers, both formative and summative. An elementary school principal stated, "Teachers are expected to know the standards and to be expert in what they teach." To increase teacher knowledge of state standards, these principals had their teachers tie weekly lesson plans to standards that were shared among and between grade levels. Another principal stated, "Teachers in the past were working hard, just not working together. . . . You have to have a curriculum [standards] that takes you where you want to go. . . . My teachers receive a curriculum handbook that contains pacing guides, standards, rubrics, prompts, and the like." Additionally, their yearly performance plans were tied to the student benchmarking activities that were evaluated by student data and achievement targets. These [curriculum] targets were monitored by the weekly pacing schedules teachers turned in for review by the principal.

PP: Class Size Reduction Through 4th Grade

Achieving the goal of a fully successful classroom through lower class size has been a major challenge to schools. Large classrooms undermine the good intentions of teachers who have to figure out how to manage young people, rather than to develop relationships and create meaningful learning environments. Reducing the student-to-adult ratio was a critical way of enhancing student achievement opportunity in the schools we studied.

State-level policies have put in place class size reduction in the first three years of elementary schooling. But in many of the elementary schools we studied, the administration extended class reduction to the 4th grade. Not only do the 4th graders receive more instruction in smaller classes, but also Hispanic and African American students score higher on standardized test results. Fourth grade is a critical year for students as they move into the upper grades, which require more advanced critical-thinking skills. And the more time that teachers can devote to students, the more favorable the results.

Principals and teachers feel so strong about reducing the 4th grade that they forgo other curricular and personnel items to budget the additional teacher for their school (i.e., using volunteer parents rather than paid aides, limiting field trips, etc.).

OTHER SCHEDULING
AND CURRICULA PRIORITIES

Extending the school year through year-round school, summer school, or intersession to accommodate extra learning opportunities for those who need it is sometimes the prerogative of the school administration. The elementary schools in this study altered their schedules by interrupting the traditional practice of the long summer vacation.

Discontinuity in the students' academic momentum creates gaps in student performance as teachers, administrators, and parents have observed. In the schools that are not on a year-round schedule, principals organize summer school for students with special needs, or devise other means of providing additional support for underachieving students. One elementary school principal commented, "I do not have year-round school; hence, I have no intersession. However, I do extend the year by five weeks for 1st graders who were behind."

By staggering schedules, principals and teachers can increase students' academic capacity. Teachers believe that with options such as intersessions or summer school, they have an alternative to failing a student because students can utilize the summer to improve their grades.

Finding ways for teachers to avoid doing recess and lunch duty—because they are encouraged to share their instructional best practices—is innovative. Elementary school principals made it a point to include this practice as a statement of collaborative working arrangements between teachers and administrators. It was not just a matter of principals being "nice" or "accommodating." The message was not a tacit one, but, rather, an overt one: "In this school, we work together across status lines."

Summary

The fact that principals influence school achievement is undeniable. Two things are essential in understanding their role in the process: (1) to identify the specific practices in their schools, and (2) to note the underlying values that their leadership inculcates. In these elementary schools, the principals, were strong instructional leaders. Not only did their credentials and background experience qualify them to be principals but also teachers believed that their respective school was successful because of the principal's vision and common sense in leadership, support of the teaching staff, and ability to be flexible as situations demanded. Teachers described their principals as accessible, approachable, having a willingness to assist them in solving problems, and, above all, as holding high expectations for students and teachers alike.

"A culture geared for achievement" is the way one of the elementary school personnel described their school. At the top of their list of reasons why they believed students in their school scored high on achievement tests was the fact that the principal was able to manipulate the day and school year to maximize teacher–student instructional time.

The Promising Practices involving school administrative leadership create a competent atmosphere that teachers can trust. Together, principals and teachers commit to learning and change not by imposing rules from the top down but by co-creating a viable learning setting for students.

3

School Curriculum and Classroom Instruction

With the exception of progressive educational movements, schools have been historically organized to accomplish objectives and skill building through books and multiple worksheets, which students read and complete. Time after time, teachers in the schools we visited emphasized, "The curriculum and instruction are not only goals ... but also vehicles that take us where we want to go." This was a telling comment from those who plan, execute, adjust, and evaluate their learning programs on a regular basis. The components of what these schools considered their curriculum involve more than texts, workbooks, worksheets, and correct student responses. The learning package is much more comprehensive. "The curriculum is visible in everything we do, how we work together, and what we use to teach, and what we do in the classroom," said one teacher. With that as the overall philosophy of the school, the components in curriculum and instruction include assessment, staff development, teacher collaboration, and classroom instruction.

Creating a culture of success involves more than just holding a yearly preservice meeting before students return to school in September. Although preservice workshops are an important part of staff development, other specific Promising Practices identified from most of the schools relate to the integrity of their schools' curriculum and instruction: The principal tests new students; student portfolios as continuous assessment; teachers trained in English language development; all teachers trained in curriculum for Limited English Proficient students; teachers hold weekly team meetings; direct-instruction approach is used; prekindergarten program organized; and daily lessons posted in the classroom.

ASSESSMENT

Test results can mean different things. The outcry against testing is that tests are biased and neither measure what they are intended to measure nor predict future success. Where testing and assessment were concerned, teachers and principals in all the schools we observed believed that they were more than functionaries in the teaching and evaluation process. They held strongly to their decision making about the tests they administered, the purpose for which they administered them, and the ongoing assessment process that best assisted them in diagnosing and planning for students' educational needs. But in support of testing are those educators and the public who believe that accountability is necessary to ensure we know if and what students are learning, and so communities can compare the performance of their local schools. The potential for schools to go astray is enormous. The schools we visited do not want tests to drive the curriculum. Instead, their concern is how schools adopt the philosophy and create policies that lead to a curriculum for all students to achieve.

In contrast to popular practice, testing for the sake of testing was replaced by ongoing assessment in the schools we observed. No one complains or is surprised when athletes practice for the big game. In fact, it is expected and supported by coaches. The coach teaches them what they need to know. And the game is a test of what they have practiced. In the schools we studied, testing what students know and/or checking to see what they will need to know is an ongoing process. All the principals were unanimous: "Use state standards . . . analyze data, graph data, and personalize the data for teachers." "Use multiple measures for consistency." "Have embedded assessments at the beginning, middle, and end of the year." "Be very data driven." For new students, it begins on the first day that they walk through the school door.

PP: Principal Tests New Students

Entering a school for the first time can be intimidating enough without having a principal administer a test to you with their first "hello." Yet principals in the schools studied found that sitting down with a new student and the parents and diagnosing what the student knew was exactly what was necessary. As one principal stated, "We can't waste any time trying to figure out what the student knows and doesn't." That is the rationale given by most of the teachers and principals we interviewed. They refuse to rely on the background information provided by the cumulative records (numerical scores that new students present upon arrival). And for many of the students, arriving on the first day with a cumulative records folder was unlikely. Age/grade placement was seen as simply insufficient for what teachers need for planning an appropriate curriculum.

Most of the principals believed that initial testing and assessment in reading and math for possible reclassification was key. They tested every new student as they enrolled. Typically, principals use the Wide Range Achievement Test (WRAT), which is a quick and general test in reading, spelling, and math. Afterwards, students are placed in the appropriate grade at that point, with parent consent. The test results point to specific educational goals. With all three present, the principal can establish an informed relationship with the parent and immediately report the level at which the student will begin the academic program.

One important reason principals assume the responsibility for administering the WRAT is that they serve as a reliable administrator of the test. Over the years, test results are more easily interpreted if the person administering the test remains constant. Thus, having the principal perform this task makes it possible to keep the introductory test process consistent.

PP: Student Portfolios as Continuous Assessment

Most tests are snapshot events that find students deficient in one or more of the following: speaking, reading, writing, computing, and creating. Portfolios are designed to provide concrete evidence of the student's strength. And where students' skills are lacking, the portfolio specifically identifies skills in a way that links them to the instructional goals and standards. The portfolio is a record of students' learning processes in a given area. Although most often teachers keep portfolios of students' writing, other subject areas can also be recorded in portfolios if teachers want a more authentic assessment of a student's work in science, social studies, language arts, and, of course, art. In addition to portfolios in those areas, teachers in the schools we observed kept portfolios in math. They preferred this form of record keeping and accountability because it gave them a way to engage parents in a more informed way about their children's work. Space availability in respective classrooms and schools sometimes precluded them from implementing an extensive portfolio accounting system.

Portfolios can include work samples, records of systematic observations, and tests taken by students. Other records include interviews with the students, anecdotal records, nonjudgmental notes of children's activity, and an inventory of the student's progress—linked to the instructional goals and grade-level standards. These ongoing collections display accountability for what was taught and how well it was learned.

A common problem in assessing educational needs of African American and Hispanic students is that standardized test data, which are usually used to identify their academic standing and achievement, are often aggregated, with all student scores reported as a single school score. The problem with this approach is that school test scores may be high in general while actual scores of African Americans and Hispanic students may be much lower and go unnoticed due to aggregation. In California, schools are now required to disaggregate the data for a student ethnic identity of 10% or greater at each school site. The schools we studied went a step further. Most teachers, and all principals, disaggregated student data on multiple levels throughout the year and used portfolios, which provided teachers and parents with a built-in system of assessment. Sharing student data between teachers typically occurs through cumulative records information, which primarily includes only standardized test scores and oftentimes unsubstantiated remarks by teachers. The system allows for a method of discussing individual student progress, achievements, and needs. Teachers feel that this method of accountability liberates them from having to rely only on standardized tests to decide how to diagnose and meet students' needs. Collectively, teachers in each school decide the length of time the students' portfolios will cover. The advantage of portfolios that teachers most often noted is that they are able to easily recognize not only student deficits but also their possibilities.

STAFF DEVELOPMENT

Staying current and informed about all aspects of teaching, learning, and parent communication is critical. "Site-based workshops are best—teachers share better and do not compete between each other while using what works in our culture," a teacher said. "Learning in our groups gives us reflective thinking time." Another teacher said, "Madelyn Hunter's Program began as a guiding program for this school. . . . We were thoroughly trained in this program and it has been the foundation of our philosophy and success with children." School principals and teachers cited continual staff development as a way to stay refreshed and able to meet the new challenges that confront schools daily. Using words such as "development" and "training" to discuss the continual learning on the part of teachers, staff, and administrators is limiting and inadequate to describe the new learning that teachers undertake. They indicate that something is being done to them to make them behave differently. But teachers and staffs we interviewed had a broader and more active way of thinking about "staff development." Teachers in our study said that they wanted to learn and stay current, but they wanted a voice in what and how to prepare themselves in new areas. "We need to be supported in learning new ways to approach our work," one teacher said. In other words, teachers in these schools assume responsibility for their growth and learning of new material. Many staffs in these schools saw each other as resources just as much as they considered attending a workshop a learning opportunity. The notion of learning from each other was critical to the strength of teaching staffs. As one junior high teacher said, "We're here for the students, but we're here for each other too." Another said, "[We are a] team—a coordinated, cohesive staff."

In the complex staff-development programs these schools design, their goal is to provide training for teachers, paraprofessionals, and volunteers on topics including writer's workshop, phonemic awareness/phonics, alignment to state standards, guided reading, and technology to enhance the language arts program.

To make staff development possible, schools build it into their budgets in a realistic way. Administrators and teachers budget funds and enough time (realistically) to accomplish what the teachers need to work on during each calendar year. In addition, the school leadership agrees on adequate release time to allow teachers and paraprofessionals to participate in educational activities that will enhance their work with students. Several school principals have teachers participating in the National Teachers Board Program. One teacher in the program stated, "We feel that teachers are professionals and should be recognized and paid as such. We think this [program] will be worthwhile for us. . . . It is a lot of work. . . . The district gives us a 15% raise when we have received the NTB qualification." A high school principal said, "The best teacher in-service happens on the school's campus to meet their specific needs. Those doing training from 'downtown' are not necessarily in the trenches meeting the school's unique challenges. In-service should be relative to the school's needs."

PP: Teachers Are Trained
in English Language Development (ELD)

One of the staff-development topics is teaching English Language Development (ELD) for English Language Learners (ELL). All teachers in the schools we studied are trained in ELD because it is understood that all teachers will at some point teach ELL students, given the high ELL populations in the respective schools. To some it seems a strange thing that a teaching staff should have to learn how to teach English Language Development to English learners. After all, if teachers just spoke English to them and made them read in English, they should be able to learn to use English. Although most students would be able to speak some degree of English within a year or two, their academic English skills would be inadequate to achieve mastery in reading and writing and to succeed in all of the other subjects taught in English only.

Many of the schools we studied had large ELL populations. They, therefore, recognized the importance of making staff development in English Language Development a priority. Paraprofessionals are part of the critical teaching partnership; thus, their inclusion in staff-development activities is essential.

Workshops that teachers and paraprofessionals attend, either at the school site or at the school district office, deal with training people in the use of specific curriculum programs. Teachers find them helpful because these schools use systematic curriculum programs in the various subjects. Training teaching staff in how to utilize materials decided on by the staff ensures they will want to be able to use them effectively. Teachers sometimes feel programs are adopted at the school, but they do not receive sufficient training in using the materials prior to implementing a program. Their training is tied to increasing student learning. "We'll do whatever is necessary to do a good job," said a teacher. This makes workshops and other staff development activities on the topic of English Language Development imperative.

These teachers, paraprofessionals, and parents also attend conferences (school, district, county, and some university programs) dealing with teaching ELL students and language-development programs. Although conferences alone do not supply the necessary support for teachers to confidently teach ELL students, they are an important supplementary form of training because teachers, paraprofessionals, and parents can meet and network with others in similar communities.

Another form of staff development that some staffs reported were visits to other schools where exemplary curriculum programs had been successfully implemented. One teacher said, "I have observed classrooms in other schools that helped me identify instructional strategies using music and move-ment to increase SAT-9 scores." Another said, "At times the very schools we visited became models for other staffs to observe."

College and university classes also make available staff development for elementary and high school staffs. Classes in leadership, classroom management, English Language Development, Spanish, Literacy, Literature, and Writing through the Curriculum were just a few of those classes noted by teachers and principals as particularly useful to their staff's learning.

The various models of staff development, central office administration, teachers, and principals explicitly reject deficit theories of education. "College begins in kindergarten and first grade," a teacher said. A principal said, "UCLA has been invaluable to us in providing research that will successfully influence our African American students who need assis-tance." Another teacher said, "You've got to make them proud of what they do—P.E.P. assemblies, poems, music, holidays, songs, rap, and so on." Most common among deficit beliefs are those that have explained school failure as something caused by the students' culture, family, or their lack of ability because of the low socioeconomic conditions in which they live. A teacher said, "Why high scores? We have systematic programs, teachable programs. . . . The principal had to fight to get materials, and teachers have to know what they are teaching. We are a multicultural faculty and we like each other." A principal stated, "Failure is not an option for any students. . . . This is why our minority students achieve."

TEACHER COLLABORATION

Respecting professional judgment on the part of teachers, paraprofessionals, and parent volunteers, and providing ways for everyone to do their job are critical leadership characteristics of the school administration. The principals at the schools we observed communicated their mission clearly to everyone in the school and were willing to share their power with the teaching staff as a way of creating a collaborative climate. These schools were organized to create a climate of collaboration. The leaders challenged teachers, staff, and parents to collaborate. Principals at all levels, elementary through high school, understood they didn't have all of the answers to deal with the educational problems plaguing their schools, but they could become true leaders by providing ample opportunities for their staff. "The most important people are the teachers. . . . The principal should recognize the strengths of teachers. . . . The principal should pick out the 'peacemakers' and they will help their colleagues teach," said a teacher. We observed how leadership gives voice to teachers' input and becomes collaboration in decision making about school policy, curriculum, and other educational practices.

Articulation around the specific schoolwide curriculum is as important as decisions about the specific commercial and supplementary curriculum. One of the things teachers do during their meetings is to disaggregate student data. Most of the principals could show us examples of exactly how staffs disaggregate student data by subgroups so that African American and Hispanic students are tracked and do not get lost in the grouping of test scores. By locating these students' scores appropriately, teachers can plan realistically for students, particularly those who need the most attention. "Together, we set the goals that we want our students to achieve," said one elementary teacher. Teaching staffs are pragmatic, for as one high school teacher described it, "We collect that data, and don't just put it aside. We analyze it and use it to design appropriate programs for each student." And another teacher stated, "This means that together we have to work hard if we want our students to achieve."

PP: Teachers Hold Regular Team Meetings

Teacher collaboration is a top priority among the staffs of the schools we observed. Typically, curriculum is an issue of turf between teachers at a school site. But in the schools we visited, teachers used their planning time to optimize coordination of the curriculum to maximize student learning. An open communication system enabled teachers to meet weekly, and as one teacher emphasized, "We don't just work together; we work hard." In one school, the staff admitted to the fact it took them a long time to build trust with each other. Feeling and working as a team require a high commitment to respecting each other's input and negotiating to reach a decision that is most suitable for each student's learning. "We [teachers] collaborate together to examine scores, share ideas, and meet with our coaches."

One of the outcomes of weekly teacher grade-level meetings is the decision to maximize the morning hours of the instructional day. Teachers in the elementary schools found that these early hours were the optimal learning hours for most students, and they agreed to hold them sacred. The initial hours of the day were reserved for reading, writing, and math. Although this seems to be common sense and quite traditional in the order subjects have been taught in most schools, all teachers in the elementary grades believed that by emphasizing this as a team, they could protect it from any interruptions by other school activities that might interfere or disturb those periods.

Both teachers and principals adamantly believed that all morning of the instructional day should be devoted to reading, writing, and math. As one elementary school principal put it, "All morning is devoted to reading, writing, and math. . . .

They have to get in everything else later." Another emphasized, "Uninterrupted instructional time."

Unfortunately, in some schools where the low socioeconomic groups and African American and Hispanic student populations are high, teacher conversations in meetings or in the lunchroom emphasize the students' academic deficiencies. Markedly different from tradition are the teaching staffs in the schools we studied. Here, teachers addressed the deficiencies in the school curriculum, which may catch up with students in subsequent grade levels.

Teachers decided on the agenda for their weekly meetings, whether they were grade-level or entire school-level teacher meetings. There they reviewed school activities and ensured they did not interfere with the academic program. In one school, teachers looked forward to lunchtime because they could eat together. During this time, they discussed how curriculum programs work in their classrooms and shared with each other the strengths and weaknesses of each program. The focus was always for the purpose of modifying it. "We do analyses of various sub test scores . . . to supplement the curriculum for our particular students," said a teacher. Teachers are intent on adjusting materials and tailoring them to the students' needs.

Principals reported that being able to select a competent and committed teaching staff of their own sometimes took years. Even once they got their staff in place, natural attrition always threatened a school. With the inevitable turnover of staff, every school has some teachers with more experience than others. And in these schools, the more experienced teachers teamed up with novice teachers to share professional strengths. As one teacher stated, "If you're going to join the club, you have to do it our way—pacing, same homework packets, lesson plans, and so on . . . or else you move on. Our teachers do it our way."

INSTRUCTION

If instruction is well designed, then testing should be a natural step in the learning process. Classroom instruction should be aimed at preparing students to demonstrate their critical knowledge of reading, language arts, writing, mathematics, and other subjects. Teachers continuously plan, evaluate, and readjust the curriculum used in instruction. "We take the test results and use them to plan curriculum for the following year," said a teacher.

PP: Direct-Instruction Approach Is Used

What teachers called "direct teaching, the 90 minutes of their morning instructional day," initially sounded like a throwback to the teacher-centered "basic skills" days when every student desk faced forward to the front of the classroom. In front of the chalkboard stood a teacher with chalk in hand, calling on students to answer questions so that she could evaluate them as "right" or "wrong." But when we walked in the classrooms and observed carefully, directed teaching came alive. The classrooms were not uniform at all. From early grades through high school level, we found dynamic, vibrant, and well-organized classroom instruction taking place. As one principal stated, "Empower to grow without fear."

On the classroom walls hung colorful artwork and student writing, and the desks were arranged in small-group clusters. But the students didn't occupy the seats. They sat up front near the teacher who instructed through story or computations on the board. The lessons were congruent with the reading and math programs, which in the early grades was usually Open Court, a reading and language arts program, and in the upper grades, Scholastic Read 180 program was used, an intensive reading-intervention program. A key feature of direct instruction involved question-and-answer exchange by the teacher that allowed every student to have a turn at responding. Teachers expected every student to get involved in the direct-instruction morning period. For example, elementary school teachers called on every student before giving students a second turn at responding to questions. Therefore, it is impossible for students to sit passively and hide from the teacher. Teachers tailored questions for each individual student. They revealed students' knowledge while specifying subsequent steps in their academic program. This allows for variance in addressing student ability. A teacher emphasized, "All students count." In this way, all students were verbally engaged in direct instruction. The level of student enthusiasm was exemplified by this direct-instruction process.

On this topic we need to note that, like every other promising practice, this one does not stand alone. In other words, these schools do not promote skill-based, teacher-centered teaching by relying exclusively on teacher-directed whole-class instruction. Directed teaching has received a great deal of criticism within many segments of the educational community. The way teachers in these schools utilized directed teaching is interrelated with the rest of the schools' organization, consistent leadership, staff development, teacher collaboration, and strong community partnership.

For teachers, principals, and parents in the noted schools, math, reading, and language arts take center stage. This makes staff decisions about the schoolwide curriculum a high-priority topic of negotiation. With reference to instructional materials and allowing teachers to have a voice in what they feel is more effective, one principal said, "First you have to identify the problem, then take steps to solve the problem. When I arrived, I found that the children could not read. I chose the Sullivan Program Reading materials. This program takes small steps. Sullivan helped the school to improve from a passage rate of 3% [when she began as principal] to 68% four years later." This principal then allowed a young teacher to teach the DISTAR reading program. Soon, a few other teachers joined her, but most preferred Sullivan. There was also some experimentation with other material, but this principal did not find this material to be as effective as the Sullivan material. All of the other teachers now teach a single program, Open Court. This principal enabled her teachers to try different approaches until a consistent program was found to raise student achievement.

PP: English Language Development (ELD) Is Taught Schoolwide

The purpose of teaching English Language Development (ELD) in every classroom is to ensure that ELL students have access to the core curriculum. Not only is the English language necessary for ELL students, but teachers must also emphasize learning to think critically, using higher-level thinking skills in all areas.

The English Language Learner (ELL) remains in the classroom for English instruction. The students receive support from a teacher assistant who stays in the classroom with them. Teacher assistants are trained by the teachers they work with and also receive specific training through the local colleges and through workshops during the school year. Specialists provide assistance for non-English-proficient students. The time period for pullouts is just a brief 6 to 8 weeks, after which the students then remain in their respective classrooms for all English instruction. Pullouts are limited and done only in the afternoon.

Principals often commented, "The most important people are the teachers." But the principals' leadership in executing curriculum and instruction occurs daily in the attention and support they give to teachers in ensuring they teach to their goals. They train teachers to use existing materials, observed in the classrooms. As one principal said, "You require lesson plans every week, even if you can only read a few each week." Teachers write complete lesson plans linked to school goals and the state learning standards. And English Language Development is central to student achievement. Thus, ELD plans appear on all of the teachers' weekly lesson plans.

PP: A Pre-K Program Is Organized

Students planning to attend kindergarten must attend a prekindergarten program. A prekindergarten program is organized in the elementary schools we observed because the principals and teaching staff expected the incoming kindergarten students to be as prepared as possible when they entered school. Twice a week for the entire year prior to entering kindergarten, students participate in a prekindergarten program.

Some schools house a child care program on campus. This allows parents and children to become familiar with their neighborhood school, personnel, and the expectations that teachers hold for them. If a prekindergarten program is not organized in a given school, some effort is made to prepare incoming kindergarten students. In several schools, the leadership organizes a formal prekindergarten program. One elementary school staff, for example, holds a prekindergarten orientation meeting in March. A packet of learning materials including the school handbook is given to each parent. As one principal described it, "We conduct a prekindergarten assessment before the school year ends in June. . . . The specific student's diagnosed learning packet is given to parents and they are told the instructional packets are the things you need to work on with your child before school begins in fall." Most of the elementary schools did pre-packets for their entering kindergarten students. And for those kindergarten students not ready for 1st grade, several schools created a pre-1st grade. A teacher stated, "We created a 'junior' 1st grade for kindergarten students not ready to move on."

PP: Daily Lessons Are Posted in the Classroom

The classroom setting is just as important for students as teachers, books, and bulletin boards, comprising an invaluable component of the instructional day. Classroom fixtures such as posters listing the class daily lessons provide a clear path for students to follow. We observed in most of the schools at all levels that when the students enter the classroom each morning or after each recess, they know to look up, take their seats, and look to the front of the room for instructions. Without wasting a minute in waiting for the teacher's attention for directions, they know how to self-direct and begin their lessons. Teachers tie the daily lessons to the grade-level curricular objectives, so every day students know exactly how their daily lessons lead them toward their subsequent goals. Posting the activity guide on the board provides consistency and requires discipline. A teacher stated, "We have goals posted in each room. Daily goals are posted. Goal setting is spoken about a lot to staff, students, and parents."

Posting the daily lessons is part of the direct-instruction concept. Given what is expected of the students, it is quite the opposite of the passive learning associated with teacher-led instruction. It has elements of self-directed learning because students take responsibility for their learning.

SUMMARY

Supporting and training the human capital in the entire school takes high priority for the schools we observed. The curriculum programs are flexible to the extent they are negotiated among teachers. The point is the program does not drive the instruction, but, rather, the students' needs drive the teachers' collaboration and curriculum choices. Making the students' needs central released staffs from the internal competition that sometimes flares around materials, resources, and overall school mission. How to accomplish this is a total school effort. It is where all of the sectors meet: the principal, teachers, para-professionals, parent volunteers, as well as alignment of the curriculum and classroom instruction. Caring for their students and each other collegially supports the grade-level and school-wide decisions made. From the most general school goals to the individual classroom goals, the principal, teachers, volunteers, and paraprofessionals work together in a committed way to build learner responsibility and independence in their daily discipline.

4

Family and Community Connections

Prior to the 1960s, most schools were neighborhood schools. They were a pivotal social center of the community they served, blurring the school–home cultural divide. Historically, the relationship between parents and teachers has been a complex one. Although much has changed in the way families relate to schools, some things remain the same. Before students step into their kindergarten classroom, and even through the years after they complete their time in school, they learn from their parents. Too often this relationship has been something referenced only when issues concerning students from culturally diverse or working-class families are in question. In those cases, the family has been mistakenly blamed for the academic underachievement of culturally diverse students. The parental role in the African American and Hispanic students' lives often ignores the fact that, historically, schools have been organized on the cultural premise of congruency between predominately Caucasian parents and the teachers who replicated their values, beliefs, and language in the classroom. Acknowledging this frequent cultural gap between families and schools, we need to recognize that neither schools nor families can relinquish the educational role to the other.

The schools we studied have a strong relationship with their community and the families of the students they teach. As one parent described, "I attend English language instruction and our class is full. . . . [I am] learning how to teach reading. . . . I am learning the sounds here and my kids learn the sounds there [in class]." How a school communicates to the respective community and families occurs within a context of these specific practices:

- Schools provide free breakfast.
- Homework is assigned.
- Correspondence to parents is sent in two languages.
- Schools provide assistance for parents.
- Students are assigned work during intersession.
- Parents are involved in schools.
- School curriculum includes parents.

SCHOOL–HOME COMMUNICATION

Since the turn of the past century, vehicles such as the Parent Teacher Association (PTA) have primarily focused on organizing social functions and fundraising. In many schools, the PTA has given way to School Site Councils (SSC) and other types of parent–teacher policy forums where parents are informed about the school's events, test scores, budget, and curriculum programs. In turn, parents provide input and support as the school requires. This form of school-policy parent involvement has been criticized by community members for isolating many parents from participating in the school. If schools hold parent meetings during hours that parents work or if the meetings are held only in English when other languages are prominent in the community, the message relayed is, "Your input is unimportant to the school." Some schools train parents to participate in policy-level school-improvement committees. Although some are able to participate in the

SSC-type meetings because they know the language and have the time required to make policy decisions, others cannot get involved in this way. This makes other forms of school–home collaboration imperative.

Building school–home connections for the purpose of strengthening student academic achievement is a strong incentive for principals and teachers in the schools we studied. They have learned through experience that they cannot achieve the academic goals for the students independent of the family unit.

Ordinarily, times and places of connection between families and schools occur at structured events where the school defines the interaction of the people involved. In such settings, educators assume a position of knowledge over the parents or community members. This results in parents having to adhere to the school culture to support their children in school-related tasks.

Typically, principals and teachers communicate with parents through written notes, on the phone, or verbally in meetings. Internet e-mail and informal meetings over a cup of coffee are used to "hear what is on their [parents'] minds," a teacher said.

PP: Students Wear Uniforms

Whether students should wear uniforms to school has been a major issue in some communities, requiring a joint decision on the part of the school, unions, the parent community, and the students. The efforts of principals and teachers to reach parents have strongly influenced decisions regarding school uniforms at all levels. This is especially true in California; California state law prohibits requiring uniforms in public schools. Teachers endorse uniforms because they believe uniforms help in disciplining students. "I wear navy and our logo daily. . . . [It] goes with our uniforms," one elementary school principal said. A high school principal stated, "Magnet schools [like mine] can require uniforms. Discipline is important. Uniforms are important because we're all wearing the same 'ugly' clothes. [It helps us to] focus on what we are learning, not on what we are wearing."

This argument used by schools and communities favoring students wearing uniforms is that it places all students on an even plane while removing the stigma of clothing status. Administrators and teachers in these schools attribute the decline of discipline problems to the standardization of the dress code. Educators and parents have found that wearing uniforms has eliminated social competition among students, allowing them to concentrate on their academic work.

Additionally, the colors selected for school uniforms are not those usually associated with neighborhood gangs. Hence, students in such neighborhoods are not likely to be attacked en route to or from school simply because their parents inadvertently purchased jackets, sweaters, or pants featuring a "gang" color. Many parents in southern California attended parochial schools in other countries, where they were required to wear uniforms to school. Consequently, there were multiple reasons why parental support of school uniform policies was easy to obtain.

PP: Correspondence to Parents
Is Sent in More Than One Language

Principals in both the elementary and secondary schools know the value of communicating with the community in their language. The principals in our study realized that communicating with parents in their respective language has improved school–home communication. Not only is this gesture one of respect, but it is also logical. If one is genuinely interested in informing, engaging, and interacting with another, then it follows that it be done in a language the other understands. Creating the school–home relationship as a partnership means that schools need to find every possible way to communicate with the community and the students' homes if they expect collaboration. Something as simple as using the home language communicates how important schools consider the parents' role to be in the school–home partnership. When schools send correspondence only in English, knowing that families in their community have different home languages, they are saying, "We don't think you are important enough for us to communicate with you in a language you understand." Excluding the community's language(s) reinforces that the schools intend to work alone without the input and support of the families. Sending every letter, note, and announcement in the students' home languages, according to the leadership and teachers in the schools we observed, takes a great deal of time and commitment, but it "gets results," said a principal. By that, schools meant they could expect cooperation from the parents because the parents were well informed. Schools made communicating with the community such a priority that they kept this in mind when hiring bilingual front-office personnel, paraprofessionals in the classroom, teachers, and recruiting volunteers. Including the community in such a critical way meant that the school leadership had to ensure that translation services for the school were included in their budget planning.

Using the parents' home languages in correspondence and in school meetings, as well as in parent conferences, establishes a collaborative relationship between the people who need the most information about the students. Two-way communication between schools and the home, once forged, becomes a durable structure for exchanging information by mail or face-to-face. As one principal stated, "We have to know how to talk to them [parents]. It is important that they do their parts at home: make sure students know that school is important, do their work, behave, and eat well before coming to school."

PP: Schools Provide Free Breakfast

Whether schools have a free breakfast program is not only a school matter but also one involving the needs of the entire community. Some parents are unable to feed their children a healthy breakfast before sending their children to school. If students are not well fed, they're unable to concentrate and, therefore, their academic performance suffers. Feeding students a free breakfast can become a political issue for some schools if the community favors the program, but the schools find that it is too costly to rearrange their cafeteria and busing schedules. In one of the schools studied, this conflict was negotiated with the community, with the schools agreeing to provide a free breakfast for the students only during the weeks of standardized testing on the SAT-9. Although the schools could not afford to make a free breakfast program available to all students during the entire school year, they compromised by providing students a good start on those days that were particularly stressful.

SCHOOL ACTIVITIES IN THE HOME

Whether parent involvement works depends on whether the relationship between parents and school staff is not only school centered but also home centered. That is, the school goes home every day with the students through the homework and emotional residue (both fun and accomplishment through hard work) of their day at school. In the home setting, parental input into their children's schooling is a complex issue. Many parents have not completed school in the United States. Essentially, such parents are unfamiliar with the way to access resources to help their children excel. One parent said, "I attend workshops called 'Partners in Print' to help me learn to read in English . . . and to read with my child." Nevertheless, parents supply strong emotional support on a day-to-day basis by listening to their children talk about their days in school; discussing conflicts with teachers and peers; and, of course, encouraging their children verbally in their academic work, sports, extracurricular activities, and social life.

Although their work goes on behind the scenes, there are more visible ways parents attempt to help their children in the home. They assist students by supervising their homework, reading to the young ones, and signing off on special work that needs to be returned.

PP: Homework Is Assigned

Schools typically assign homework to students for the purpose of enhancing their academic performance. Yet homework has sometimes been the source of conflict between parents and schools. Sometimes homework could be said to create a greater gulf between students and the school because it assumes that family members possess a certain level of academic preparation to assist their children. The schools we studied consider homework a high priority because they have seen evidence that it is an important part of the students' learning, thus benefiting academic performance. Most of the schools assign homework five nights a week. Teachers told us, "Part of the homework has to include reading lessons." They link the schoolwide reading program to daily homework assignments. Some elementary schools have specific policies that require the assignment of a minimum of 30 to 40 minutes of homework in reading, math, and spelling from Monday through Thursday. Teachers at all levels develop homework in their grade-level team meetings. "We are all on the same page. . . . It helps us focus on our students," said a teacher. They consistently review the students' grade-level needs in the various subjects, and together they discuss how students perform the assignments.

Another way that schools support the students in completing homework is by opening the school library at 7:15 A.M. for browsing and completing homework. This also solves the early-drop-off problem faced by many working parents.

Some schools hire a part-time paraprofessional or assign a classroom teacher assistant to spend some time in the classroom and one hour in the library. As part of the homework policy, upper grades through senior high school provide up to two hours of homework tutoring before or after school for students needing academic support.

PP: Schools Provide Assistance for Parents

How can parents play the role of teachers every night when they did not go to college for teacher training? Helping parents to create a home environment that supports the learning their children receive in school is an important component and promising practice of the schools we studied.

What, how, where, and when to do homework may seem to be commonsense issues to most, but for those parents unfamiliar with the school system and its requirements, such issues can be the source of regular nightmares. For that reason, parents are given assistance on how to check homework and how to help their child do the homework. A principal said, "Parents do translating orally and in print. What we do here crosses over to the next school level [middle school]. We volunteer to baby-sit while parents are tutored. We feel good about that."

At the beginning of the school year, parents receive copies of the academic standards expected of all students. An elementary school parent said, "I learn teacher methods to help children do their homework." That way, parents are not playing a guessing game about what the school expects of them and their children. Because classroom lessons are tied to the general state academic grade-level standards, parents can check their children's homework against the standards and know that they're on track.

Grade-level meetings are held for parents. With all the grade-level teachers together, parents can ask questions on the expectations held for their children. They can observe if their child is being pushed unrealistically or not enough. Parents can see how all the grade-level teachers care enough for their child to design classroom lessons and homework for every student in that grade level, offering total support to meet the standards.

One school had a Web site for parents. Parents with computers at home can log on and find up-to-date announcements, schedules, and upcoming events. Parents can also use the Web site as a way to communicate with their child's teacher or other school personnel.

Making homework a contract with the student and the parent has worked for many schools. The approach is, "Here is how you can help," said the teachers. "Parents sign off on all homework." Even if parents do not sit down with their children to do the homework, by having to sign off on it they must read it and ask the child to explain what they have done. It is a way to review homework every night.

PP: Students Are Assigned
Work During Intersession

In the year-round schools, students typically take a three-week break from their academic studies, but not in the schools we visited. Teachers in those schools sent home a well-prepared packet of homework with each student, which teachers organize in their grade-level meetings. The homework relates to the grade-level standards, the class curriculum, and the state-testing objectives.

Parents agree to assist their children in completing their homework and ensure the work is returned when classes resume. Those parents who work during the day when students are on break arrange to leave their children at daytime centers. There students receive tutoring or assistance with their intersession homework packets.

Upon returning to school from the intersession, teachers carefully review all of the assigned work, not only for correctness but also for understanding.

Homework packets are not only assigned to students during intersession. In May of each year, elementary schools in this study assessed those students who are scheduled to begin kindergarten. Students receive the readiness packet to work on during the summer.

PARENTS IN SCHOOLS

Schools expect parents to be visible in the school. Their presence shows that they care about their children's education. Yet many differences exist in the nature of parental involvement between elementary and high school. Elementary parents tend to get involved more than high school parents, because of the closer relationship younger children have with their parents. "I [elementary school principal] think parent involvement is vital. It makes them feel like they are a part of the school, empowers them, and gives them ownership."

Many traditional activities have made parent and teacher exchanges possible. On the more conventional end are the annual "Back to School Night," "Open House Night," "yearly conferences," "award ceremonies," and PTA meetings. Although these school activities claim to bring many parents out for these one-time events, they fail to sustain an ongoing collaborative relationship between teachers and parents throughout the year. Teachers believe they need to stay in constant contact with parents to maximize their students' achievement. Therefore, stronger and better-defined school-family-community connections are enabled through programs in the schools we studied.

PP: Parents Are Involved in Schools

From elementary to high school, parents are expected to be involved in their children's schooling. A high school parent said, "I help proctor tests and [help] teach test-taking strategies." A junior high parent said, "I help write grants to get more money for specific projects." An elementary parent said, "I was in-serviced to help with the SAT-9 testing and test-taking strategies."

Parents would be hard-pressed to say they genuinely do not care about their children's education, yet they often lack specific knowledge on how to help. School expectations of the parents and the way they can participate is a culture of its own. That is, schools typically define the way parents should communicate with the school and the type of activities that support the school's standards. How parents participate varies depending on their skills, time availability, interests, children's needs, and their level of confidence in relating to school personnel.

Much is made of the need for parents to engage in schools, but some school personnel believe that parent involvement can interfere and that schools need to set limits. One principal commented, "This topic has been exaggerated.... Parents can get in the way at school so it is important for the school to work with the parents." Another principal stated, "It is very important for them [parents] to attend back-to-school activities.... They have always played a key role in fund-raising . . . and, especially, it is important that they do their parts at home: make sure students know that school is important, do their homework, and come to school well groomed."

Parent involvement is imperative for student achievement. Finding ways to build a strong partnership between parents and schools can take many forms. No single type of parental involvement works better than another, but what is required is commitment on the part of both the parents and the school to work together for the students' benefit.

PP: Parents Are Trained to Assist in the Classroom

Having parents volunteer to assist in the classroom requires specific training from teachers and other school staff. Teachers train parents in how to help students to succeed in academic tasks and in ways to assist and volunteer in the classroom. Parents assist in specific activities including tutoring individual students in math, reading, writing, or spelling. Teachers instruct parents on how to teach and how to use the specific classroom curriculum for the respective classroom. Teachers also recruit parents to assist in administering standardized tests. "We [parents] do hands-on curriculum in test-taking strategies tied to homework for the students," said a parent. Given the priority placed on test taking and creating a comfortable environment for students to work in, it makes sense that teachers used trained parental volunteers for assistance. A high school principal said, "Parents are being asked to help track where our graduates are going, to help establish some kind of track record of our students."

Teachers want tight control of the way in which parents can assist teachers. Even for activities that are less academic, such as posting student work, teachers feel accountable for the quality of adult–child interaction that occurs in the classroom. After all, teachers do not work alone. In the elementary schools, teachers work more as a grade-level team and every student's academic achievement is a primary concern of the grade-level team. Thus, training volunteers to assist in classrooms is very important.

PP: School Curriculum Includes Parents

A truly effective parent–school partnership means inform-ing the parents of the school curriculum, and, in these schools, parents are an important part of that curriculum. How school personnel include parents may range from delineating parental responsibilities in the home to demonstrating how parents can check homework. Teachers conduct training workshops for parents by grade level, especially for the non-English-speaking parents, to instruct them in ways to work with students at home on reading, writing, and math, and ways to assist their children in homework. As one teacher indicated, "We provide training for parent volunteers for our reading program." Additionally, teachers teach parents English-language skills for the sole purpose of helping parents to be better able to work on homework with their children.

Several schools in our study used the Waterford Software Program for kindergarten and 1st grade, which teaches parents how to assist their children at home. Interested parents attend the training workshops and teachers actively recruit all parents and encourage most of them to attend.

In the higher grades, including middle and high school levels, the schools involve the parents differently. Although involving parents of older students is generally challenging for principals and teachers, the schools we studied made a special effort in the middle and high schools to stay in con-stant communication with parents about the students' progress. Regardless of the students' achievement level, the schools kept parents informed about their children's academic standing through written contact. Teachers met regularly to discuss student progress and to help design workshops for parents on how to assist their children at home, or to find tutors for their children. They also participated in parent–school partnership organizations at their respective schools, where parents share ideas of ways to reach their teens; offer support and information about academic concerns, college applications, and financial aid for college; and tips on dealing with difficult school personnel.

The schools we studied saw themselves as a viable part of the community at large. An African American parent said, "We have many volunteers here. We feel comfortable here. We intermingle socially. The kids see us here and that rubs off on the kids. They think school is important." Just as schools perceived the parents as part of the students' support system, they also view other community sectors as part of that advocate team for the student. School–parent partnerships often involved community agencies to collaborate with the school organization. By coordinating parents with community businesses, family agencies, and local colleges and universities, the high school–parent partnership is strengthened. At the African American high school, this was especially evident in their on-site training of students for future medical field professions that were part of the community collaboration with a university medical hospital. Parents could be trained as well. An elementary school principal said, "We have a real need to work cooperatively with the community. We have magnet, private schools nearby to which the parents have access financially and otherwise. So we work with the Chamber of Commerce, UCLA, business merchants, and so on, to see that our program meets many needs and expectations."

SUMMARY

Strengthening connections between the home, school, and community is a fundamental part of the schools we visited. Communication between these different sectors happens on a regular basis, and every avenue is utilized until the parents are reached.

Building social capital in the family through parent involvement is an important component in fostering a strong learning environment for students. The family's attention to their children's education at home *and* at school is the impetus for supporting students' access to the resources they need to succeed.

5

From Promising Practices to Action

Some reports try to relate students' low test scores to low socioeconomic status, non-English-speaking environments, or, particularly, membership in certain ethnic groups. How we have chosen to understand this issue has greatly influenced public schooling over the past 40 years.

High achievement for all students is a goal most in the nation can agree on. But from national policy leaders to teachers, there is not agreement on the best strategies to effectively educate all students, especially poor and minority students. Local school districts and school leaders need to find their own pathways to effectiveness. We believe that reflecting on practices that have worked in high-achieving schools with high-minority student enrollments and applying those Promising Practices to other districts and schools can result in *all* students moving to higher levels of achievement.

The schools we have studied have proven that schools can change against all odds and make learning possible for all students. What makes change possible is not a magic act. It is accomplished consciously and conscientiously through slow and deliberate work. Collectively, school leaders, teaching staff, parents, and community agencies roll up their sleeves and take responsibility for the day-to-day job of schooling the next generation. Systematic, committed hard work is what it takes on everyone's part to support students' academic success.

Since Horace Mann, public schooling has survived because it has changed. In systematic ways, how students learn can shift the historical trend—that poverty leads only to low scores—to giving public schools hope.

WHAT WE NEED TO ASK OURSELVES

Every Promising Practice raises specific questions to consider. The most important question is: Who is responsible for change? That responsibility rests on any person with any stake in the future of the next generation. That includes school leaders, teachers, parents, district administration, school board members, and the entire community. People in every sector of school life need to ask themselves certain questions in order to proceed. What follows are some questions to help guide the actions you choose to take.

Questions for School-Site Leaders

The "can do" attitude exhibited by the principals we visited was no surprise. Clearly, all saw themselves as strong leaders and were ready to tell us why. The following quotes exemplify that attitude: "School administration and teachers support the school goals for the child and his/her education." "I can't just be a paper pusher and sit in my office. My vision has to be their vision." "Principals have to be service oriented and know the reading and math curriculum." "Principals are instructional leaders who help with curriculum. They're in the classroom and visible in the school."

About School Leadership

1. Does your school have a mission statement that has been designed by you and the teaching staff?

2. How often do you visit each classroom for the purpose of observing the instructional process?

3. Is the morning instructional period free of interruptions? What is done through leadership policy to protect classroom instructional time?

4. Do you have a flexible school recess and lunch schedule, allowing for maximum teaching time and time for teachers to talk with each other?

5. Do you take a teacher's yard duty whenever possible?

6. How do you hold teachers accountable for implementing the academic standards?

7. Do you disaggregate student data and ensure your teachers understand and work with these data frequently?

About the School Curriculum

1. What type of assessment do you require of new students who arrive at your school?

2. What school plan exists to prepare students academically prior to entering kindergarten? Entering middle school? Entering high school?

3. How is a student's academic process assessed on a regular basis throughout his/her career in your school?

4. How does the school staff-development plan prepare teachers to teach students who speak a language other than English?

5. Do you facilitate regular teacher grade-level meetings in your school?

About the Classroom

1. How familiar are you with teacher instructional methods in the classroom? How do you support them to develop their teaching strengths?

2. How much emphasis do you place on English Language Development in the curriculum?

3. Do you require teachers to post their lesson plans in their classrooms for everyone to see?

4. How frequently do you discuss each teacher's instructional plan with the respective teacher?

5. Do all curriculum programs provide schoolwide continuity for students?

6. Are teachers trained to implement the state-adopted curriculum in reading, math, science, and language arts?

7. How do you hold teachers accountable for teaching to the state-level standards and the high school exit exam?

About the Community

1. How important is parent and community involvement in your school?

2. What type of parental involvement do you encourage in your school, policy decisions, and classroom?

3. How are parents integrated into the school's academic plan? How are standards and testing expectations explained?

4. Does the school have an organized group where parents and school personnel can meet to make joint decisions?

5. Are school uniforms an issue in your school and community? Where do educators and parents stand on the issue?

6. Does all of your school correspondence go out in the respective home language of all parents?

7. Does the school offer a school lunch program for those who qualify?

8. In what ways do you support parental involvement in the home?

9. How much homework do students in the school receive nightly?

10. What type of parent educational workshops does your school organize for parents to assist their children with academic work?

11. How do you relate to grade-level plans so students can continue studying through their intersession and vacation periods?

Questions for Teachers

The school culture is shaped by more than the strong beliefs of its teachers. In our interviews, teachers shared their own professed commitment: "First of all, we have the principal's leadership. It took a long time to build the trust." "The principal has high expectations of us." "We're here for the kids. We don't have competition between teachers (or grades) here." "We're more like a family, working together rather than just taking directives from the top down." "We all set high goals for the students."

About School Leadership

1. Have teachers been included in formulating a mission statement for the school?

2. What is that school mission and how does it guide your daily instruction?

3. How often do your school leaders visit your classroom for the purpose of observing instruction?

4. How much feedback do you receive from them (the school leaders) after the visit?

5. When you need to meet with a parent or a student, does the principal assist you by taking your recess-duty responsibility?

6. Does the principal ensure that you have uninterrupted instructional time when teaching the core curriculum subjects?

7. What kind of lesson plans tied to standards and use of disaggregated student data does the school leadership expect of you?

About the School Curriculum

1. How are new students assessed when they arrive at your school?

2. What type of academic plan does the school have to support prospective kindergarten students? Prospective middle school students? Prospective high school students?

3. How are students in every grade level assessed academically and on a continuous basis?

4. How prepared are you to teach students who speak English as a second language?

5. How much planning do you do with other grade-level teachers? With other academic content teachers?

6. How does the school principal hold you accountable for promoting school standards in your daily instructional program?

About the Classroom

1. How prepared do you feel to meet the academic challenge of all your students?

2. How does the school staff-development plan assist you in that challenge?

3. What instructional methods do you employ to teach the various subjects throughout the day?

4. How important is English Language Development in your classroom? In the grade levels across the school? In the academic content levels across the school?

5. Are you required to post your lesson plans in your classroom? Are your lesson plans tied to the standards? Are your lesson plans tied to the high school exit exam?

6. Does the principal discuss your instructional program with you and with every other teacher?

7. Do you consider the school administrator(s) to be instructional leaders in the school?

About the Community

1. How do teachers involve parents in their classrooms?

2. How much communication do you have with the parents from your classroom?

3. What kind of school plan exists for teachers in your school to meet with parents for the purpose of joint decision making?

4. What teacher efforts are involved in training parents to assist their children with homework?

5. What type of training do parents of students in your classroom receive to support their children's academic progress?

6. Do you send notices to parents in the home language of the student?

7. Do you discuss the matter of school uniforms with parents in your class? With other teachers?

8. Does your school offer a free breakfast and/or lunch program for students who come to school hungry?

9. What kind of academic plan do you have in place for your students to ensure their continued studying during intersession or vacations?

Questions for District Administrators

Strong administrative leadership by the principal, especially in regard to instruction, is a basic assumption shared by all educators. District administrators ensure that each school's mission is clear and tied to the districts' goals and state standards, and that principals are strong instructional leaders. Implementation of board policy requires district leaders to set the level of expectation.

About District Leadership

1. Is there a district strategic plan? Does it address content and performance standards for instruction?

2. Does the district set the expectations that schools will improve student performance on high-stakes examinations?

3. Does the district make specific commitments to assist schools to improve student performance?
   A. Does the district permit principals to have flexibility in the allocation of instructional time to ensure emphasis on standards assessed by state tests?
   B. Does the district have a priority in the allocation of fiscal and other resources that support school efforts to improve student performance?
   C. Does the district make provisions for staff development for site administrators, teachers, and other instructional personnel?
   D. Does the district offer recognition for personnel who succeed in improving student performance on standards-based tests?

About School Leadership

1. Does the district select school-site leaders and reward those who carry out the agenda to improve student performance?

2. Does the district support school staff in their efforts to address student performance?

3. Does the district monitor the performance of its administrators and take corrective actions if there is a need for program improvement?

4. Does the district communicate to parents and the community the plans and accomplishments of school leaders who effectively improve student performance?

About the Curriculum and Classrooms

1. Does the district assist schools with communication and training to implement curriculum standards and student expectations?

2. Does the district provide means of assisting teachers with instruction, such as coaches and staff development?

3. Does the district assist the schools with the assessment program in terms of test administration and the analysis of student scores?

4. Is there a high priority for district expenditures related to acquiring up-to-date textbooks, ample instructional materials, and state-of-the-art equipment for instruction, including those that are technology based?

About the Community

1. Does the district have a strategic plan? Does it address long-range projections of trends the community might demand in the future? Are there ways parents and others in the community are encouraged to participate in programs at school sites or in district activities?

2. Does the district have ways to assess how parents and others view the public education services provided in the district?

3. Does the district use a variety of means to inform parents and the community about school needs, accomplishments, and recognitions?

4. Is there a district Web site? Is there a district newsletter? Are Board of Trustees actions routinely communicated to parents and the general public?

Questions for School Board Members

Local leadership includes school board members, who are charged with implementing the goal of educating all students. The connection between policy development and implementation strategies, especially for under-performers, mandates that school board members encourage their administrative teams toward new levels of accomplishment.

About School Leadership

1. How do you support the school district and individual schools to implement a strong community-involvement program?

2. Does the school district have a position or policy about school uniforms?

3. What is the school board's position on using the home language to communicate with parents and the community at large? How are the schools supported to encourage communicating in people's respective language?

4. What is the school board's position on principals as instructional leaders? State standards? State testing? High school exit exam?

About the School Curriculum

1. How does your school board's policy on learning and curriculum translate to the daily reality of learning in a school site and in the classroom?

2. Does your school board have a position on testing and assessment in the schools? What is the premise on testing new students? On doing continuous assessment throughout the year?

3. What is the board's position on teaching students whose home language is not English?

4. How often do you visit schools?

About the Classroom

1. How often do you visit school classrooms while they are in action?

2. How do you stay informed about the daily instructional process?

3. When you visit a school, what do you look for in a classroom? What do you expect to see?

About the Community

1. As community members, what is your position regarding parental involvement in the schools?

2. How do you support the involvement of parents in their children's education?

Questions for Parents

Parents play an important role in their children's learning; school personnel strongly supported that. In their words: "In school, we don't rely on parents to do our job, but we do appreciate it when they support their children as much as possible." "If the parents can see exactly what you're doing, they understand why their child needs rest and breakfast, and [they] know how to help with homework." "Teachers give it their all and we want the parents to understand that."

About School Leadership

1. What is the school mission?

2. Do school leaders visit the classroom? How often?

3. Do school leaders take yard duty during recesses?

4. Do school leaders design the school recess and lunch schedule to allow flexible time for teachers to communicate with each other informally?

5. Do principals protect the morning instructional hours for teachers and students to focus strictly on the academic subjects?

6. How are teachers evaluated? Are lesson plans with clear objectives and standards required?

About the School Curriculum

1. How do principals assess new students when they arrive in the school? Are they assessed so they can fit into a curriculum designed for them?

2. Before students enter kindergarten, middle school, or high school, does the school have a plan to assist them academically? What kind of plan exists?

3. How is your child's academic progress assessed on a continuous basis in the classroom?

4. Are classroom teachers trained to teach students who speak limited English?

5. How much communication and planning occurs between teachers in the respective grade levels or academic content levels at this school?

About the Classroom

1. When was the last time you visited your child's classroom?

2. How important is English Language Development in the school curriculum?

3. How much English Language Development is taught across the grade levels?

4. When parents visit the classroom, are the teacher lesson plans posted in a visible place, making their daily activities apparent?

5. Does the principal in your child's school discuss the teacher's instructional plan with each teacher?

About the Community

1. How are you involved in your child's school?

2. Does the school have an organized parent group that allows parents to express their views and receive clear information about school matters?

3. Where do parents and educators stand on the issue of school uniforms for students?

4. What efforts are made for both parents and teachers to address the question of uniforms?

5. Does the school send correspondence to parents in the language (respectively) spoken by the students' families?

6. How much homework is assigned to your child? How much support do students have to complete their homework? How are you supported to help your child complete his or her homework?

7. What kind of training do parents receive to maximize the academic support of their children?

8. How does the school ensure that students continue to study during intersession and vacation time?

SUMMARY

The responses to these questions will indicate the work ahead if you find that certain practices are not in place. How change is initiated or how it evolves in any one school can take many different routes. But one thing is certain: Maintaining effective learning settings in a school requires the total support of school personnel, central district administration, school board members, the community, and parents.

It is everyone's responsibility to stay vigilant and promote the high standards that uphold learning and academic success. Disaggregating data by poverty through grade levels for all districts in reading and math, whether urban, rural, or suburban, is a critical first step in addressing the achievement gap, especially among Hispanic and African American students. Low grades and test scores lead to course selections and inadequate preparation for college, especially for large numbers of minority students. But the various sectors cannot act alone, independent of each other. All sectors involved must reach out to create partnerships that respect one another's positions.

Resource A

School-Site Information

		API 1999	Rank 1999	API 2000	Rank 2000	English Language Learners	Free & Reduced Lunch	Hispanic	African American	Full Credential	Read +50% Star 2000	Math +50% Star 2000
Inglewood												
Bennett/Kew	K-5	776	9	775	8	28.80%	79.90%	47.4%	51.90%	76%	2,3	2,3,4,5
Highland	K-5	717	8	761	8	35.90%	78.10%	40.0%	57.70%	34%	2,3	2,3,4,5
Hudnal	K-5	718	8	781	8	46.40%	9.50%	66.4%	31.60%	47%	2,3	2,3,4,5
Kelso	K-6	824	10	808	9	34.20%	79.40%	53.4%	44.40%	70%	2,3,5	2,3,4,5
Parent	K-8	638	6	683	6	.70%	22.40%	7.2%	90.20%	59%	2,3,4	2,3,4,5*
Payne	K-5	706	7	748	7	71.90%	95.10%	88.7%	9.20%	50%	2,	2,3,4,5
Downey												
Imperial	K-5	691	7	722	7	36.40%	60.50%	73.7%	2.40%	79%	2,3	2,3
LAUSD												
Lane	K-6	737	8	749	7	36.50%	85.20%	91.9%	0.60%	83%	2,3,5	2,3,4,5
Cowan	K-5	737	8	744	7	1.90%	31.80%	9.5%	57.31%	85%	2,3,4,5	2,3,4,5
HS King-Drew	10-12	630	6	601	4	45%	40.40%	21.8%	71.80%	71%	0	0*
Oakland												
Grass Valley	K-6	681	7	712	7	1.20%	24.80%	1.2%	97%	86%	2,3,5	3,5
Kaiser	K-8	714	7	724	7	4.20%	16.90%	8.8%	54.40%	100%	2,3,4,5,6	3,4,5,6,7*
Howard	K-6	641	6	681	6	0.90%	58.90%	0.6%	94.60%	90%	4,	2,3,4,5

Resource B

Brief Overview
of Bibliography

Interwoven connections between effective school and instructional leadership practices are where principals demonstrate their ability to "walk the talk." Effective school and instructional leadership practices have been defined by many researchers to mean strong administrative leadership; clear objectives; safe and orderly environment; test-to-curriculum alignment; close monitoring of pupil progress; coordination of instruction; and high expectations for student achievement (Bell, 2000; Carey, 2001; Cohen, 1981; Edmonds, 1979, 1982; Haycock, 1999, 2001; Johnson, 2000; Johnson, 1999, September 2000; Munitz & Papalewis, 1999; Owens, 2001; Papalewis, 1997, July 1999; Reyes, 1999; Rossow, 1990; Samuel, 2000; Schomoker, 1999; Smith & Andrews, 1989; Watkins, Lewis, & Chou, 2001).

Hanson (1991) criticized effective school literature because it lacked a conceptual framework due to its corelational framework; had limited ability to link elements of school structure; emphasized good management and not good teaching and learning; and focused the teaching of effective schooling on case study approaches. Likewise, studies of principals and how they spend their time are in contradiction to sound instructional leadership. The discrepancy (Kowalski & Reitzug, 1993) is described as a disconnection between how principals are evaluated and the practices required to ensure that they are seen as leaders. Principals lose their jobs for being poor managers, not for being poor instructional leaders.

Beginning in the late 1960s, Weber (1971) showed that high-achieving school leaders with high-poverty students exhibited strong instructional leadership; high expectations; orderly climate; and a curriculum focus placed on reading.

Edmonds (1979, 1982) wrote that, primary to all else, students acquiring basic school skills should precede all other school activities; pupil progress should be monitored frequently; and school resources should be diverted away from all other business that is not directly connected to student achievement. He (Edmonds, 1979) believed that it was a school's response to family background that was key to believing that poor children can achieve. He felt it was not family background so much as it was within a school's organizational structure and management processes that enabled or disabled instructional activities leading to effective student achievement. He defined effective schools as schools that helped all students achieve high test scores due to (1) a schoolwide emphasis on improving instructional skills; (2) a climate that supports learning; (3) a teaching–learning process that is monitored frequently; (4) a school that is safe and where school discipline and a respectful climate are maintained; (5) a school where all personnel set high standards for every student; (6) a school culture that shares high expectations through shared values and norms; and (7) an especially strong principal to provide structured classroom leadership. Cohen (1981) echoed these and added that teacher expectations must be that all students, regardless of family background, can achieve.

Wolk (May, 2001) felt he shattered the 1960s myth that high-performing schools cannot be found with students who are poor, urban/rural—based on research done in Kentucky during the 1990s. His findings for effective school practices included the following: curricula are aligned across grade levels and topics; teachers cross boundaries to work and plan together, share stories, techniques, and ideas that focus on each student; teachers use student test scores to modify their teaching; and principals get parents involved in their child's learning. And finally, adding to this list of effective practices, Johnson (April 1999) feels successful schools don't accept excuses, and that everyone at the school site needs to feel valued, appreciated, and know that they belong.

The instructional leader research (Carey, 2001; Firestone & Wilson, 1985; Johnson, 2000; Owens, 2001; Rossow, 1990; Smith & Andrews, 1989) focuses on high expectations and respect. The school principal places a high priority on curriculum and instruction; involves faculty in decision making; keeps the school safe and orderly; protects instructional time; and ties the schools objectives to curriculum standards and testing benchmarks.

There are a number of recent reports that collect school success stories focused on high-performing and/or diverse schools. These include California Assembly Select Committee on Low Performing Schools, Chair, Darrel Steinberg, March 13, 2001, *Against All Odds: An Examination of Outstanding Academic Performance in High Performing Schools;* Johnson's *Equity-Driven, Achievement-Focused School Districts: A Report on Systemic School Success in Four Texas School Districts Serving Diverse Student Populations,* 2000; Johnson & Asera's *Hope for Urban Education: A Study of Nine High Performing, High Poverty Urban Elementary Schools,* 1999; and Haycock's *Dispelling the Myth: High-Poverty Schools Exceeding Expectations, 1999 Report of the Education Trust.*

Resource C

Research
Methodology

ABSTRACT

Exemplary urban schools that defy the downward
achievement trends came to our attention. There ensued
a yearlong research study to understand what made the
difference in 13 identified high-performing African American
and Hispanic majority schools. After extensive interviews and
observations, we found these school principals and teachers
believed and expected that all students were capable of
learning and went about creating high-achievement learning
environments.

THE SCHOOLS: SELECTION AND DESCRIPTION

Thirteen schools in California were chosen for demographic
purposes. Also, California had recently initiated a comprehensive accountability system for its public schools. The
accountability system begins with a school-by-school score
to a ranking system called the "Academic Performance
Index" (API).

Selection: The Academic Performance Index (API)

The API is the cornerstone of the Public Schools Accountability Act (California Senate Bill 1X) signed into law in April 1999. This law authorized the establishment of the first statewide accountability system for California public schools. The purpose of the API is to measure the academic performance and progress of schools. It is a numeric index that ranges from a low of 200 to a high of 1000. To calculate the API (California Dept. of Education, 2001), individual student scores in each subject area on the Stanford 9 test are combined into a single number to represent the performance of a school. The national percentile rank (NPR) for each student tested is used to make the calculation. The percentages of students scoring within each of five NPR performance levels (called performance bands) are weighted and combined to produce a summary result for each content area. Summary results for content areas are then weighted and combined to produce a single number between 200 and 1000. This single number represents the school's API score. For more details, see www.cde.ca.gov/psaa/api/yeartwo/growth/apiinfo.pdf.

For the purposes of this study, a statewide rank was used that compares an individual school's API to all of the schools in its grade-level category statewide. With respect to all elementary, middle, or high schools, the rank is interpreted as follows:

9 or 10	well above average
7 or 8	above average
5 or 6	about average
3 or 4	below average
1 or 2	well below average

The state has set 800 as the API score that schools should strive to meet. The median score for 1999 for elementary school was 629, for middle school was 633, and for high school was 620. For 2000, elementary school was 675, middle school was 657, and high school was 633 (CDE Press Release, January 17, 2001).

Relevant to this study is that the API not only targets schools as a whole, but also scores and targets are reported for schools with significant ethnic and socioeconomically disadvantaged subgroups. California's accountability system requires that all numerically significant groups (10% of the student population) of students within a school grow academically. This requirement makes a strong statement that achievement of all students in a school is important. No student should be left behind (CDE Press Release, January 17, 2001).

The thirteen schools are representative of all schools in that they did not focus on urban schools or only low socioeconomic schools. The focus was on the distribution of the African American and Hispanic schools that were over 50% in population and ranked above the median baseline score. According to WestEd (October 1999) in a preliminary handout for a conference held in Sacramento on high-performing, high-achieving poverty schools, the distribution of schools that were over 50% African American students found that on the statewide ranks, no school in California ranked ten, only one school ranked nine, two schools ranked eight, two seven, and 11 ranked six. This is from a total of 125 schools with only 16 ranking at six or higher on the API. Likewise, the distribution of schools that were over 50% Hispanic students found that on the API rankings, two schools in California ranked ten, four schools ranked nine, 12 schools ranked eight, 41 ranked seven, and 98 ranked six (total 157 schools ranked six or higher on the API). This is from a total of 2,209 schools with over 50% Hispanic students across the ten API ranks (WestEd, October 1999). In contrast, the distribution for schools with over 50% Caucasian students had 587 schools rank ten, 517 schools rank nine, 517 schools rank eight, 417 schools rank seven, and 305 schools rank six. This is from a total of 2,728 schools with 2,343 ranking six or higher on the API. The total percentage of Caucasian schools that ranked from the low of one to five on the API was 14%, in contrast to African American schools at 87%, and Hispanic schools at 93%. These percentages indicate that 87% of predominately African American and 93% of predominately Hispanic schools in California are failing schools (using the API definition). Additionally, this displays the disproportionate number of failing schools, given California demographics of 47% of the schools' population are Hispanic, 12% are African American, and 37% are Caucasian.

Description

Initially, five elementary schools were chosen to visit. These schools were selected using two criteria: More than 50% of the student population was either Hispanic or African American, and that the school, using the Academic Performance Indicator (API), was at least as high as the statewide average score (ranked seven to ten). Following the visits to the five schools, eight more were chosen for visitation to broaden the research to include junior high and high school, and especially to verify what were emerging Promising Practices. Consequently, the selection criterion was adjusted to include overall rankings statewide of six and seven for junior and senior schools, respectively. These schools represented public schools in California located in both the northern and southern parts of the state.

The majority of the schools visited were inner-city schools. These were schools situated in high-poverty areas, surrounded by low-income housing. The housing surrounding these schools were gang- and drug-ridden. Other schools we visited were brand-new or recently refurbished sites, with lawns and playgrounds full of permanent equipment, which are more indicative of suburban communities.

The two top-ranked schools were in the same inner-city school district. One was ranked ten on the API—the only predominately Hispanic school (53%) in the state to rank ten. The other was the top-ranked African American school in the state (51%) with an API of nine. The combined African American and Hispanic student populations in each of these two elementary schools was 98%. Both student populations were high-poverty schools—approximately 80% of the students participated in free and reduced lunch programs.

Of the remaining 11 schools, eight were elementary (K–5 or K–6), two were K–8, and one was 10–12. These 11 schools had the sense they were high-achieving, but most had not been visited for their success. Their delight in having us point out their success to them was very pleasant. They told their stories with different perspectives, but all shared many of the same practices. Of these 11 schools, four were 50%+ Hispanic and seven were 50% African American.

Of the total 13 schools, only two were staffed at 90% or higher with fully credentialed teachers. The two schools staffed with the most number of emergency teachers were at 47% and 34% fully credentialed. Two had 50%+, four at 70%+, and three were 80%+ fully credentialed. As their stories were told in these schools, having emergency teachers was not seen as the terrible crisis we normally read about, especially with current research on the subject. In these schools, both the principals and teachers viewed these emergency permit teachers as "opportunities," with more life experience and desire to be teachers. Some principals considered them better than fully credentialed teachers and more enthusiastic and willing to take direction.

These 13 schools had the following baseline statewide score rankings: 10—one Hispanic elementary school; 9—one African American elementary school; 8—two Hispanic elementary school, two African American elementary schools; 7—two Hispanic elementary schools, one African American elementary school, one African American K–8 school; 6—three African American schools (elementary, middle school, and high school).

THE RESEARCH: TRAINING AND OBSERVATIONS

A total of nine team members were trained. A team of five researchers went to each school site. Of the team members, four visited all the schools. Besides the two authors (superintendent from a suburban school district and university professor), three of the researchers were current district office directors or recent past principals. Most had worked in both urban and suburban schools with 30 or more years of experience in teaching and/or administration.

These research team members were trained on qualitative participatory research methods. They were taught to do structured interviews, examine documents, and observe classrooms. They were asked to visit schools that were distinguished in their proven success with high-performing students in primarily African American and Hispanic majority schools. The team members included six African Americans and three Caucasians. Their goal was to identify what role leadership played in the outcome of the students' high achievement. API and other test information were discussed.

The three activities the team members were trained for were: interviewing, examination of relevant information, and observation. Interviewing guidelines were emphasized, such as: ask the same questions of each person you are interviewing; take notes of what is said, not how you feel about it; explain the question to ensure they understand what you are asking; and watch for nonverbal clues and note those. Examination of relevant information meant the team members were to gather and review copies of each school's mission statements, codes of student conduct, rules to parents, newsletters, curriculum statements made by teachers to parents, and the like.

Observation was discussed in terms of gathering a schoolwide sense of the culture of the school. For instance, What were the interactions among the adults and students; evidence of school pride; evidence of diversity of school students; evidence of how students are supported; schools rules and their enforcement; school cleanliness, safety; evidence of a library and resource labs; students in uniforms; counselors, social workers, nurses; and the overall condition of the school site?

OBSERVATIONS

Prior to the interview, school principals were sent a letter telling them we wanted to discuss their school's success on the SAT-9 and API ranking. The principals were asked to provide a minimum of one hour for their interview and 20 or 30 minutes for several teachers on their staff. If possible, meetings with parents were to be arranged. The general topics we asked them to consider were: their background as a principal/teacher; their philosophy for high student achievement; their priorities for the school; changing roles/aspects in the school as a result of the high API ranking and SAT-9 scores; slogans they use to describe their beliefs about their school and its students; and other information they would like to share.

We were warmly greeted into the 13 schools. The two inner-city elementary schools had received many visitors and were quite prepared to tell us their story. These two schools knew they were unique because of their success with Hispanic and African American students.

Principals and teachers were asked in the interviews to describe their background and how they had come to be at this school. They were asked to describe their successful school practices and to what measure they felt the success was attributable to them. Sample questions were:

1. To what do you attribute students' high achievement on the SAT-9?

2. Reflect on the following topics, as to which are most critical to achieving your school's success: ongoing assessment; instructional time; direct instruction; role of the principal; role of the teachers; teacher training; intersession/summer school; ethnicity and race of students; and role of the parents.

3. Describe the successful teaching model you utilize at your school and what its key components are.

4. What are your goals for continued student success?

5. Slogans often describe strong cultural beliefs. What's your slogan? For example, high-performing, high-minority school principals have described their beliefs as "Able to work with all kids that walk through the door"; "Think kids . . . not African American or Hispanic"; and "What it takes is this . . . putting kids first

and believing all kids can learn . . . lots of hard work, a committed staff, trust, compassion, and clear standards for behavior and performance."

6. What else can you tell us that would be crucial to understanding your school's high level of student achievement?

The observation sheets were labeled "Promising Practices observed," including slogans used to describe the school, its culture and curriculum, and leadership styles seen in teachers and parents. Principals selected classrooms to visit and escorted the team throughout the tour. Meetings with parents were without teachers and administrators present.

Resource D

A Case for District Leadership

We suggest in this book that Promising Practices lead schools to intentional choices. We believe all schools, including high-achieving districts, have a stake in beginning to address educating all their students. No margin of "left behinds" are acceptable, especially for those who reject the failure of poor or minority students.

Rarely does the district leadership receive attention in the reform debates. The study did not examine district policy development, resource-allocation patterns, accountability designs, or central office directives. But it was apparent that some school programs and practices in operation were not designed or selected by each school acting independently.

Our research found in some districts (Inglewood USD and Los Angeles USD) there were clear central office directives regarding the use of certain Promising Practices. Likewise, in Oakland and Los Angeles there were parameters established by the district office allowing local school options (Oakland USD and Los Angeles USD) as long as certain academic performance goals for students were being met.

The most direct example of district office leadership that translated into higher student performance was found in Inglewood. When asked why so many elementary schools in Inglewood had statewide rankings of 7, 8, 9, or 10, an elementary principal said, "It was because of the leadership of the former superintendent who asked all of his schools to adopt practices found in his top two performing elementary schools."

In the case of King-Drew High School, the interview with the high school principal suggested that the district (LAUSD) played a strong role in issues related to student access, enrollment opportunities, and resource allocation, while allowing the school to institute local practices such as a mandatory requirement for student uniforms, student discipline expectations, and expansion of community partnerships.

The Oakland Unified School District was in transition at the time we visited. The governance structure had changed to permit the mayor of the city to appoint three of the ten school board members. A new superintendent had just been hired. A principal stated, "We [school-site personnel] are quite satisfied with our current reading program, but anticipate that the district will direct us to change [to the Open Court] programs unless we can document increased improvement in student performance using our current reading program." The administrators and teachers acknowledged their apprehension was not based on any understanding about the program; rather, it was a fear of what the change itself might bring.

Conversations in these school districts made us realize that it may not be what the central office directs that matters most with people at school sites, but how they perceive these new directives will affect them. Our book has focused on successful high-minority and mostly high-poverty schools with very intentional practices. In this Resource, a case study is presented as an example of how one successful suburban school district chose to use the Promising Practices.

CUSD Ethinicity Comparison for SAT 9 2000 District Reading

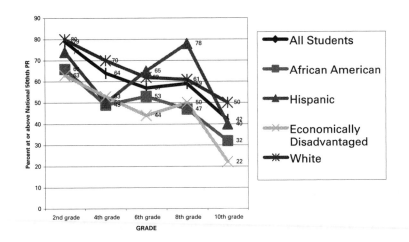

A CASE STUDY

Using our research, a suburban district discovered, when data were disaggregated by poverty levels and ethnicity, that a high number of Hispanic and African American students were under-performing the dominant Caucasian population. The average API for this district (in 2000) was 749, the highest average district scores in the county.

This district's superintendent stated, "We were motivated to undertake some of the Promising Practices because of the relatively lower achievement of specific groups of students, yet [I realized] virtually all the practices affect all students."

Disaggregating data was not a common practice for Center Unified School District until a couple of years ago. Prior to that time, the district reports were the average scores of all students in each grade and at each school. The relatively low performance of certain ethnic groups was masked because, taken collectively, minority students account for less than 40% of the district.

Schools with students performing between the 1st to 39th percentile were directed to develop intervention strategies.

The district superintendent, using the questions provided in Chapter 5, asked the district-instructional staff, and then from a pared-down list, its site-level principals to review the Promising Practices and identify (1) those practices they were already doing; (2) those practices they believed required district oversight for all schools to begin to participate in; and (3) those practices they were not doing but believed they should be doing that were school-site specific. This "reflective" process brought about the following changes:

1. For the lowest group of students in the 1st to 20th percentile, the district planned for more instruction time to occur, such as after-school tutoring and instruction for secondary students. The district funded an extra teacher to conduct intersession classes for students when they would normally be off track (students and their teachers attend school for 60 days then get a 20-day break [intersession]). Students who scored below the 20th percentile needed more instructional time, smaller classes, and instruction targeted to their specific needs. Schools were not expected to fund staffing and instructional planning alone. They had the full support of the school district.

2. A critical part of district support was to acquire and give assistance at the school-site level in disaggregating data and then to fund the extra instruction needed.

3. The need to provide time for teacher collaboration was a Promising Practice that was not a part of the district's organization. For the elementary schools, the district hired the equivalent of three teacher positions for each elementary school to allow teachers to have 3 hours once a week for 25 weeks to engage in teacher collaboration. This provides opportunity for teachers to meet and plan for the lower-achieving students. The three new teachers for each elementary school provide instruction in music, visual and performing arts, physical education, and science. This district's intent was to encourage these teachers to watch the

identified students to ascertain if they exhibit special talents or interests in performing arts.

4. The implementation of teacher collaboration at the junior and senior high schools was focused on colleagues sharing strategies that lead to better performance by students, especially those who had traditionally not done well on benchmark assessments.

5. In times of tough negotiations with the collective bargaining units, these local dollars spent on special programs were viewed as competing with employee salary raises. At this point, the school district has been able to attend to both the union and curricular needs. In general, special new funds for these new programs are a small part of the total budget. Foreseeable challenges include being able to obtain better productivity out of the general fund budget.

6. Securing and maintaining the support of the school district's board of trustees is critical. There were instances when a few employees did not like a particular district or school strategy and tried to undermine board support. In that regard, cabinet members or school staff were encouraged to provide board updates in monthly reports or at board meetings. This has proved effective in maintaining the commitment of the trustees because new efforts may require change in attitude and patience until the wrinkles are addressed.

References

Bell, J. (January 21, 2000). *Revised draft: Report on high-performing, high-poverty schools symposium.* Sacramento, CA: HP2 Symposium Report.

California Department of Education. (2001). *Academic Performance Index, API.* Sacramento, CA: California Department of Education, California Department of Education Policy and Evaluation Division. www.cde.ca.gov/psaa/api/yeartwo/growth/apiinfo.pdf.

Carey, L. M. (2001). *Measuring and evaluating school learning* (3rd ed.). Boston: Allyn & Bacon.

CDE Press Release. (January 17, 2001). *2000 academic performance report for California schools.* Sacramento, CA: California Department of Education.

Cohen, M. (April/May 1981). Effective schools: What the research says. *Today's Education, 58*–61.

Edmonds, R. (October 1979). Effective schools for the urban poor. *Educational Leadership, 37* (1), 15–24.

Edmonds, R. (December 1982). Programs of school improvement: An overview. *Educational Leadership, 40* (3), 4–15.

Firestone, W. A., & Wilson, B. L. (1985). Using bureaucratic and cultural linkages to improve instruction: The principal's contribution. *Educational Administration Quarterly, 21* (2), 17–30.

Hanson, M. (1991). *Educational administration—Organizational behavior.* Boston: Allyn & Bacon.

Haycock, K. (2001). Closing the achievement gap. *Educational Leadership, 58* (6) On-Line. http://www.ascd.org/readingroom/edlead/0103/haycock.html.

Haycock, K. (1999). *Dispelling the myth: High-poverty schools exceeding expectations.* Washington, DC: The Education Trust.

Johnson, J. A. (2000). The identification of correlates impacting effective curriculum revision and educators' perceptions of the pursuant project effectiveness. In P. M. Jenlink (Ed.), *Marching into a new millennium: Challenges to educational leadership* (pp. 272–285). Lanham, MD: The Scarecrow Press, Inc.

Johnson, J. F. (September 2000). *Equity-driven, achievement-focused school districts: A report on systemic school success in four Texas school districts serving diverse student populations.* University of Texas at Austin: Charles A. Dana Center.

Johnson, J. F. (April 15, 1999). Lessons learned from successful schools. *Achieving Schools Conference.* The University of Texas, Austin: Charles A. Dana Center.

Johnson, J. F., Jr., & Asera, R. (1999). *Hope for urban education: A study of nine high-performing, high-poverty, urban elementary Schools.* University of Texas at Austin: Charles A. Dana Center.

Kowalski, T. J., & Reitzug, U. C. (1993). *Contemporary school administration: An introduction.* New York: Longman.

Munitz, B., & Papalewis, R. (1999). Society's requirements for K–12 confront higher education. In R. A. Roth (Ed.), *The role of the university in the preparation of teachers* (pp. 108–128). London: Falmer Press.

Owens, R. G. (2001). *Organizational behavior in education: Instructional leadership and school reform* (7th ed.). Boston: Allyn & Bacon.

Papalewis, R. (1999). Effective, efficient, and innovative teacher training. In California Citizens Commission on Higher Education (Ed.), *Connecting the vital parts: A California roundtable discussion on effective, efficient, and innovative teacher training* (pp. 4–8). Los Angeles, CA: California Citizen's Commission on Higher Education.

Papalewis, R. (July, 1999). *Teacher credentialing in California.* California Association of Student Financial Aid Administrators.

Papalewis, R. (1997). The comprehensive public university confronts the reform of K–12 education. In N. H. Gabelko (Ed.), *Cornerstones of collaboration* (pp. 12–18). Berkeley, CA: University of Berkeley.

Reyes, P. (1999). Creating student-centered classroom environments: The case of mathematics. In J. D. Scribner & A. Parades (Eds.), *Lessons from high-performing Hispanic schools: Creating learning communities.* New York: Teacher's College Press.

Rossow, L. F. (1990). *The principalship: Dimensions in instructional leadership.* Englewood Cliffs, NJ: Prentice-Hall.

Samuel, C. (2000). *No excuses: Lessons from 21 high-performing, high-poverty schools.* Washington, DC: The Heritage Foundation.

Schomoker, M. (1999). *RESULTS: The key to continuous school improvement.* Alexandra, VA: Association for Supervision and Curriculum Development.

Senate Bill 1X. (April 1999). *Public schools accountability act.* Sacramento, CA: California State Legislature.

Smith, W. F., & Andrews, R. L. (1989). *Instructional leadership: How principals make a difference.* Alexandria, VA: Association for Supervision and Curriculum Development.

Steinberg, D. (March 13, 2001). *Against all odds: An examination of outstanding academic performance in high-performing schools.* Sacramento, CA: California State Assembly, Assembly Select Committee on Low-Performing Schools.

Watkins, W. H., Lewis, J. M., & Chou, V. (Eds.). (2001). *Race and education: The roles of history and society in educating African American students.* Needham Heights, MA: Allyn & Bacon.

Weber, G. (1971). *Inner-city children can be taught to read: Four successful schools.* Washington, DC: Council for Basic Education.

WestEd. (October 1999). *Improving education through research, development, and service.* Oakland, CA. *www.wested.org/html.*

Wolk, R. (May 2001). Perspective: Mission: Possible. *Teacher Magazine. www.edweek.org/tm/html.*

Suggested Readings

Coleman, J. S., Campbell, E. Q., Hobson, C. J., McPartland, J., Mood, A. M., Weinfeld, F. D., & York, R. L. (1966). *Equality of educational opportunity.* Washington, DC: U.S. Office of Education, National Center for Educational Statistics.

Delgado-Gaitan, C. (1990). *Literacy for empowerment: The role of parents in children's education.* London: Falmer Press.

Delgado-Gaitan, C. (2001). *The power of community.* Denver, CO: Rowman and Littlefield.

Fullan, M. G., & Stiegelbauer, S. (1991). *The new meaning of educational change.* New York: Teacher's College Press.

Helfand, D. (April 30, 2000). Inglewood writes book on success. *Sunday Report, Los Angeles Times. www.latimes.com/news/state/updates/lat_ing1000430.htm.*

Jencks, C. S. (1972). The Coleman report and the conventional wisdom. In F. Mosteller & D. Moynihan (Eds.), *On equality of educational opportunity* (pp. 3–66). New York: Random House.

Little, J. W. (September 1990). The persistence of privacy: Autonomy and initiative in teachers' professional relations. *Teachers College Record, 91* (4) 509–530.

Orocozo, L. *Educating diverse populations.* (2001). Irvine, CA: Coastline College & University of California. *www.coursewise.com/disciplines/education/orozco.html.*

Sarason, S. B. (1995). *School change: The personal development of a point of view.* New York: Teachers College, Columbia University.

Skrla, L. (Spring 2001). *The influence of state accountability on teacher expectations and student performance.* In UCEA, The Review, XLII, 2.

Viadero, D. (March 22, 2000). Lags in minority achievement defy traditional explanations: The achievement gap. *Education Week, 19,* 1, 18.

Index

Academic Performance Index
(API), 12, 69–72, 73, 74,
75, 79
Andrews, R. L., 65, 67
Asera, R., 67
Assessment, on-going, 20–21
Assessment, Promising
Practice for:
new student testing by
principal, 5, 21–22
student portfolio, 6, 22, 23

Back to School Night, 44
Bell, J., 65
Bulletin board, use of, 6, 12,
13–14

California Department of
Education, 70, 71
Carey, L. M., 65, 67
Center Unified School District
case study, 79–81
Chou, V., 65
Class size reduction, 7, 16–17
Classroom, guiding questions
about, 51–52, 54, 58–59, 60
Classroom assistant, 45
Cohen, M., 65, 66
Community, guiding questions
about, 52–53, 55, 56–57, 59,
60–61
Counselor, on-site, 8

Curriculum, 19–20:
assessment in, 20–23
guiding questions about, 54,
58, 60
parental inclusion in, 46–47
staff development for, 23–27
teacher development for,
27–29
visual display of, 13, 14

Deficit theory of education,
26–27
Direct instruction, 6, 30–31, 34
District administrator, guiding
questions for, 55–57
Diversity, 8, 9
Downey, school-site information
for, 64
Dress code. see school uniform

Edmonds, R., 65, 66
Effective school:
definition of, 65, 66
practices of, 67
Effective school literature,
criticism of, 65–66
Elementary school:
structured/high-expectation
practices for, 5–7
time maximization practices
for, 7–8
Emergency Permit teacher, 9

English Language Development
    (ELD), 6, 25–26
English Language Learner
    (ELL), 25–26, 31–32
Escalante, Jaime, 9

Failing school:
    characteristic of, 4
    predominantly African
        American, 71–72
    predominantly Hispanic,
        71–72
    traditional blame for, 10, 26,
        35–36, 49
Family/community connection:
    parent in school, 43–47
    school activity in home, 40–43
    school-home communication,
        36–40
Firestone, W. A., 67
Free breakfast, 6, 39–40

Guiding questions:
    about classroom, 51–52, 54,
        58–59, 60
    about community, 52–53, 55,
        56–57, 59, 60–61
    about school curriculum, 54,
        58, 60
    about school leadership,
        50–51, 53, 56, 58, 59

Hanson, M., 65–66
Haycock, Kati, 65, 67
High-performing and/or
    diverse school, reports
    on, 67
Homework, 6, 7, 40–43, 46

Individual Education Plan
    (IEP), 14
Industrial model of
    schooling, 14

Inglewood:
    district office leadership in,
        77, 78
    school-site information for, 64
Instruction, classroom
    aim of, 29–30
    traditional, 19, 30
Instruction, classroom,
        Promising Practice for:
    daily lessons posted, 33–34
    direct instruction approach,
        30–31
    English Language
        Development
        schoolwide, 31–32
    prekindergarten Program,
        5, 7, 32–33

Johnson, J. A., 65, 67
Johnson, J. F., 65, 67

Key activity, 15
King-Drew High School, district
    office leadership at, 78
Kowalski, T. J., 66

LAUSD, school-site information
    for, 64
Leadership:
    definition of effective, 65
    district office, 77, 78
    guiding questions
        about, 50–51, 53,
        56, 58, 59
    in high-achieving school,
        66, 67
    purpose-intended, 1, 3
Lewis, J. M., 65
Lippicott Reading
    Program, 31
Los Angles Unified School
    District, district office
    leadership in, 77, 78

Madelyn Hunter Program, 23
Magnet school, 9, 37, 47
Mann, Horace, 11, 50
Math, 6, 28
Methodology, of study:
    interview, 74–76
    school description, 4, 8, 72–73
    school selection, 69–72
    team member training, 73–74
Mission, of school, 6, 12–13, 27
Munitz, B., 65

National Teachers Board
    Program (NTB), 24

Oakland, school-site
    information for, 64
Oakland Unified School District,
    district office leadership in,
    77, 78
Open Court, 6, 30, 31, 78
Open House Night, 44
Owens, R. G., 65, 67

Papalewis, R., 65
Paraprofessional, 24, 26, 27
Parent, 24, 26, 27, 33
    grade-level meeting for, 42
    guiding questions for, 59–61
    traditional in-school activity
        by, 43–44
    Parent, in school, Promising
        Practices for
    classroom assistant
        training, 45
    inclusive curriculum,
        46–47
    parent involvement, 44–45
Parent-Teacher Association,
    36, 44
"Partners in Print," 40
Performance band, 70
Portfolio, student, 6, 22, 23

Prekindergarten Program, 5, 7,
    32–33
Preservice workshop, 20
Principal:
    attributes of strong, 18
    guiding questions for, 50–53
    role in influencing school
        achievement, 18
    scheduling/curricula priority
        innovation by, 17
Principal, Promising
        Practice for:
    bulletin board use optimized,
        6, 13–14
    class size reduction, 7, 16–17
    classroom observation, 8, 12,
        14, 15
    instructional time increase, 15
    school mission posted,
        6, 12–13
    uninterrupted learning time,
        5, 15
    weekly pacing schedule, 5, 15
Proficiency in English Practice
    (PEP), 6
Promising Practice,
    definition of, 3
Public education,
    criticism of, 2
Public Schools Accountabilty
    Act, 70
Purpose-intended
    leadership, 1, 3

Reading, 5, 6, 7, 15, 28, 30,
    31, 40, 78, 180
Reitzug, U. C., 66
Reyes, P., 65
Rossow, L. F., 65, 67

Samuel C., 65
SAT-9, 5, 6, 7, 8, 26, 40, 74,
    75, 79 (figure)

Saxon math, 6
Scholastic Read 180, 6, 30
Schomoker, M., 65
School activity, in home,
    Promising Practice for:
    homework, 6, 40–41
    Intersession work
        assignment, 7, 43
    parent assistance, 41–43
School board member, guiding
    questions for, 58–59
School Site Council (SCC), 36–37
School uniform, 6, 8, 37–38
School-home communication,
    36–37
School-home communication,
    Promising Practice for:
    free breakfast, 6, 39–40
    parent correspondence in
        home language, 7, 38–39
    school uniform, 6, 8, 37–38
Self-directed learning, 34
Smith, W. F., 65, 67
Staff development, 23–25, 23–27
Staff development, Promising
    Practice for:
    English Language
        Development teacher
        training, 25–26
    visit school with exemplary
        curriculum, 26
    Standardized test, 6, 16,
        22–23, 27–28, 45
Standards:
    checking homework
        against, 42
    increasing teaching
        knowledge of, 16
    meeting, 13–14
    posting, 8, 12, 13–14

Steinberg, D., 67
Suggestion box, student, 8
Sullivan Reading Program, 31

Teacher:
    grade-level meeting for,
        8, 28
    guiding questions for, 53–55
Teacher assistant, 32
Teacher collaboration, 27–28
    regular team meeting as
        Promising Practice for,
        5, 28–29
Teacher development, 27–29
Teacher-led instruction, 34
Test:
    achievement, 2–3, 5
    SAT-9, 5, 6, 7, 8, 26, 40, 74,
        75, 79 (figure)
    standardized, 6, 16, 22–23,
        27–28, 45
Time maximization, 4, 7, 15,
    28–29
Tutoring, 45

Vice principal, 14

Waterford Software
    Program, 46
Watkins, W. H., 65
Web site, school, 42
Weber, G., 66
WestEd, 71
Wide Range Achievement
    Test (WRAT), 21, 22
Wilson, B. L., 67
Wolk, R., 67
Writing, 28

Year-round school, 43

**CORWIN
PRESS**

The Corwin Press logo—a raven striding across an open book—
represents the happy union of courage and learning. We are a
professional-level publisher of books and journals for K-12 educators, and we are committed to creating and providing resources
that embody these qualities. Corwin's motto is "Success for All
Learners."